HER STORMS

Sheila Wingfield

Her Storms

SELECTED POEMS
1938-1977

With a Preface by
G. S. FRASER

---

*Behold, the world is full of trouble, yet
beloved : what if it were a pleasing
world? how would'st thou delight in
her calms, that canst so well endure her
storms?*

St. Augustine,
taken from Quarles' *Emblems*

DUBLIN: THE DOLMEN PRESS
LONDON: JOHN CALDER

Set in Pilgrim type and printed and published
in the Republic of Ireland at the Dolmen Press,
North Richmond Industrial Estate,
North Richmond Street, Dublin 1

ISBN 0 85105 335 1

Published outside Ireland,
except in the U.S.A. and in Canada,
by John Calder (Publishers) Ltd.,
18 Brewer Street,
London WIR 4AS

ISBN 0 7145 3674 1

Distributed in the U.S.A. and in Canada
by Humanities Press Inc.,
171 First Avenue,
Atlantic Highlands, N.J. 07716

Contents

Acknowledgements

Many of these poems originally appeared in *The Dublin Magazine, The London Mercury, Time and Tide, The New Statesman and Nation* and *The New Statesman, The London Magazine, The Listener* and *The Times Literary Supplement.* My thanks are due for permission to reprint.

No words can adequately thank Dr. Isobel Armstrong of Leicester University for selecting what she considered worthwhile from five previous books of verse and one new, unpublished, collection. I have submitted to her Draconian judgement with happiness and gratitude.

Preface

SHEILA WINGFIELD published her first volume, *Poems*, at the age of thirty-two in 1938 but the volume included many poems published earlier in periodicals and, as she says herself, 'My determination to be a poet was formed in the nursery.' In 1946, she published a long poem, *Beat Drum, Beat Heart*, of which Sir Herbert Read wrote on its publication (he had seen a newly printed copy left by his hostess in his room and it excited him so much that he lay awake all night) :

> *Beat Drum, Beat Heart*, which impressed me greatly when I first read it about two years ago, strikes me now as the most sustained meditation on war that has been written in our time. I find it difficult to think of a modern poem of equal length that so successfully maintains such a unity of style and such directness of vision.

Yet there are, I suppose, many readers today who have never heard of this poem or of Sheila Wingfield's work generally. She published other volumes, *A Cloud Across the Sun*, in 1949, and a selected volume of old and new poems, *A Kite's Dinner* in 1954. I remember reviewing this with great enthusiasm in *The New Statesman*. Four or five of the poems in it seemed to me worthy of permanent places in anthologies of English twentieth-century verse.

There was a gap of ten years between this volume and *The Leaves Darken*, 1964, and it is only recently that Sheila Wingfield has begun to write poems again. The new poems in this volume, which are shorter, sometimes slighter than her earlier work, seem to me also more delicate in texture and more subtly oblique in approach. (The long gap was partly due to an illness necessitating a series of operations; Sheila Wingfield is still an invalid, in recurrent daily pain but, in the movement of her mind and her spirited conversation, the most active invalid I have known, other than her scholarly friend John Hayward who, among his multifarious commitments, was poetry advisor to the Cresset Press and introduced that fastidious and now, alas, defunct firm to Sheila Wingfield's work.) I quote a short poem from the recent work that seems to me to illustrate that delicacy and obliqueness. This poem, *Remote Matters*, reminds me a little of the economy, the unstated implications, of Landor's wonderful last volume.

REMOTE MATTERS

As long as I can kneel to tell
Pin-eyed from thrum-eyed primroses
Or find a small cranesbill
In rough grass,
Why should I mind
If Dunwich is under the sea
With nine churches drowned.

There is not a word wasted there and the references are absolutely precise. Herbert Read spoke of the 'simple strength' and 'precise form' of the shorter poems included in *Beat Drum, Beat Heart*, and it is interesting to compare what I have quoted with two short poems from Sheila Wingfield's first volume, with its plain title, description and claim, *Poems* :

WINTER

The tree still bends over the lake,
And I try to recall our love,
Our love which had a thousand leaves.

A BIRD

Unexplained
In the salt meadow
Lay the dead bird.
The wind
Was fluttering its wings.

These, if published around 1912, would have been recognised as masterly Imagist poems in the manner of Ezra Pound or H.D. But Sheila Wingfield had in 1938 never heard of Imagism. It was her fate, and in some ways a lucky fate, to be a natural poet and to live, apart from a very few friends like John Hayward and like Ottoline Morrell in her late Gower Street days, quite outside the literary world. She sometimes deeply regretted this, but I think it helps to give her poetry its very special tone. No voice could be more individual, no personality more tantalisingly evasive.

Sheila Wingfield is something rather unusual in women poets, an objectivist. She is more interested in all the wonderful, sad, and glorious detail of the world around her than in herself; I, as a poetic introvert, preoccupied in poetry with my own feelings and sensations, and too inobservant of nature and obtuse about people to make any vivid picture of the world outside me, envy her that. This is not to say she is a poet lacking in very strong emotions, but that the emotions get expressed indirectly through her grip on the outer world. In this respect, the poet contemporary to herself she resembles is not any other woman, but an Irishman by birth who spent much of his life in England (Sheila Wingfield is an Englishwoman by birth who spent much of her life in Ireland) : Louis MacNeice.

Sheila Wingfield has, in fact, described her theory of poetry much better than I can do, as well as the range of her subject-matter :

> As for subject-matter — the Irish and English countryside and country ways in general are so deeply rooted in me that I fancy much of this blows through my work. History, archaeology, folklore and the superb economy of the classical Greeks are other influences. These tendencies came together in forming my poetic outlook. This can be stated simply. What is personally felt must be fused with what is being, and has been, felt by *others*. But always in terms of the factual. Nothing woolly or disembodied will do. The same goes for events (which are in fact emotions suffered throughout history and in

many lands). Personal dislike for amorphous description is shown by the 2,000 line poem, *Beat Drum, Beat Heart*, which compares men at war with women in love, and is in fact a lengthy psychological-philosophical piece without one philosophical expression and I fancy hardly an abstract noun in it. It attempts to sweep over whole cultures and peoples and histories — but invariably in terms of known or perhaps only suspected feelings, expressed in a way that makes such feelings recognisable by a great variety of human beings.

MacNeice, except that city ways fascinated him as much as country ways, might have said almost all these things : and his greatest poem *Autumn Journal* does sweep over 'cultures and peoples and histories' (how the Greeks are different and long ago) as well as meditating on the coming war and exploring ruined love affairs. But he has a gloss and sophistication, suiting him, which Sheila Wingfield would think it vulgar to aim at.

Coleridge wrote to the Duchess of Devonshire :

> O Lady, born to pride and pleasure,
> Where gat ye that heroic measure?

The Duchess's verses have not survived in the canon and Coleridge, no doubt, was swept off his feet like many a middle-class poet before and after by aristocratic condescension. But though born to wealth, and married to an Irish Viscount, Sheila Wingfield found no 'pride and pleasure' in her lot. Her outer social roles find no place in her poetry and her two volumes of memoirs, *Real People*, Cresset Press, 1952, and *Sun too Fast* (as Sheila Powerscourt), Bles, 1974, show her personality, as her poems do, indirectly, through the sort of person or incident that arouses her curiosity. The gardens of Powerscourt and the great house (burned down accidentally under subsequent ownership) alone sometimes touch her Muse. But a Dublin beggar can fascinate her even more.

She never goes wrong, I think, when she writes about country life; animals; pain, courage, or ecstasy. In some

moods I find this my favourite among her short poems, and
it would in my worst moments be a poem on which I could
bite like a bullet :

POISONED IN SEARCH OF THE MEDICINE
OF IMMORTALITY

When Hsüang Tsung, great emperor,
Giddy and ill, carried in a litter,
Saw the stars sway,

His conquests and his arguments
And powers, falling into fever with him,
Pulsed their lives away.

Bow to his shade. To be at rest
Is but a dog that sighs and settles : better
The unrelenting day.

Sheila Wingfield has told me that she has no philosophy, and
none is to be found in her poems : if to have a philosophy
means 'to be at rest', she is right. But there is another wis-
dom, the wisdom of passion, of the endless search for
experience and some essence in experience — whether of
death or eternity — in spite of all pain. 'Better', and Sheila
Wingfield, even swaying on a sick woman's litter, has ex-
posed herself to it, 'the unrelenting day'.

G. S. FRASER

Poems
1938

WINTER

The tree still bends over the lake,
And I try to recall our love,
Our love which had a thousand leaves.

A BIRD

Unexplained
In the salt meadow
Lay the dead bird.
The wind
Was fluttering its wings.

TRIPTYCH

From mulberry air which feels
Folded in thickness,
Her dress where she passes
Catching in spiked grasses
And glaucous aloe,
Her child and she, breathless,
Towards Egypt go.

Bleached are all noises
And brittle the mornings;
Chip of builders who cling
To golden scaffolding,
And shouts, will not drown
These tinklings and brayings
In Hierusalemes town.

Such greyness of misery
None else knows.
Three men crouch, asleep;
Still as a stone they keep :
The world in its plight
Cannot halt a cockcrow's
Curl in paling night.

YOUNG ARGONAUTS

In a small bitterness of wind
The reeds divided, as we felt
Our keel slide over stones, and smelt

The lough all round us. Soon the trace
Of shore was further than the sight
Of wildbirds crying in their flight;

But now the waves are paler finned,
The water blacker, we are blown
To somewhere strange and yet foreknown :

This is the Euxine, this the place —
Row on, row on, to catch the gold
In dripping fleece, as they of old.

HIGHLANDER

And when he took his grief
Into the gentle-breasted hills,
He felt clouds marching, and the wind
Unheeded and unheeding pass
Through smallest bilberries in leaf
And the tough mountain grass,
Until he could no longer hear
The pressing of his soul,
And prayed to be released from self, from name,

To mingle senseless with the air
Some little time. But as within his mind
The oar would not desert its thole,
To his dark courtyard back he came
Uncomforted of all his ills.

THE HOURS

I

The hill lifts off her mist, as slow
As goddesses unrobe their feet,
And over spires and rooftops cling
The flushed veils of the morning's heat;
But gradually, to and fro,
We hear a pulsing in the street,
Rattle of window and of wheel,
Or cries, or river freshening :
Brisk and seaward in their flow,
The urgent ripples make us feel
A need to hammer through the world,
Or sail to where small islands lift,
To ride beside the wind, or shift
Great rocks that once the giants hurled.

2

Noon with his compass legs will walk
Across meridians of the sea,
And for a while, watch with the hawk
A salty shrub in Tartary,
The council of the mountain crests,
A tortoise quivering a stalk
Of barley, or a man that rests
Under a Syrian almond tree;
And when the sun's unbarriered track
Reaches the downs, and from his groove
He slants his heat upon my back,
I pry through trellis of the vetch
And spotted cloverleaf, and move
A forest with a fingerstretch.

3

Look from your windows, lovers, lean
On bridges in the warm, tired air,
For now is evening poised between
Light-hearted day and the dark's snare,
Like a girl flirting in her glass
And softly letting down her hair.
The little moths in seeding grass
Flutter their life out through the field
Where starwort gleams, and as you pass,
All colours that have loudly made
A dying declaration, yield
In whispers to the very shade
Of lichen, and of sheep that browse
Dimly below orchard boughs.

4

Alone among night-scented leaves
Must Sargon's daughter, pining, tend
Her charge, the Babylonian moon;
While others, like the leaning sheaves
That now in darkness seem to blend,
Make love; it is the hour when soon
St. Jerome, putting down his quill,
Unlatches to the secret friend,
Then works, with all Judaea still;
When some will wake at horror's edge,
And women start the pains of birth;
When careful paws creep out to kill
And a bird twitches in the hedge,
While dreams smoke from the quiet Earth.

THE DEAD

1

The wind that blew the plumes astray
And bore the trumpet noise away
Has so effaced the dead
And thinned them to so fine a mist
That, harried in a drove,
They run ahead.
This wind, from barrack square
Or from the asphalt near some tenement,
Does it persist
In hinting that each mortal should prepare
To shiver in a leafless grove? —
A jealous wind, that will steal half
Of the hot meadow's reaper-clack
Which is all summer, or the night-stock's scent,
Or, on the road, a friend's laugh,
And pleases to hurl back
Smoke or broken tiles where urchins shout;
Which turns a sleeper's thoughts to untrue shapes :
A stubborn wind, that thickens till you feel
A door bang. And then memory's shut out.

2

The quiet dead,
Who were decoyed by a false tale
Of murmurings on Lethe's pebbly bed,
Have cast from them as childishness our joy
In live and woken things which yet, may now
Be part of their own foolish, constant dreams,
And are aloof from how
We long to peer behind the murk
And pantomime of bony jowl
And yew and headstone, to unveil
Their voices or their children's screams,
Or how they hummed and paused at work.

[19]

But tautly as you dare to strain
In listening, you only hear again
Hector to Aias calling like an owl,
At night, across the windy plain of Troy.

3

In spite of it, so many of us strive
With vigour, when alive,
For marks of perpetuity;
In spite of knuckle-bones that lie
In hills, grass shuttered from the light;
In spite of that Imperial road
Where warriors stand in their huge stone
And wildflowers blow about their feet; in spite
Of nothing being colder than the rain
On knees of monuments, or mute as fame
From trumpets with the angel gilt;
Though manifold can be a name
As is the wind's print on the seas
And yet will fade in libraries,
Or few as those in thymy air
Found carved on a Pentelic chair;
Though this one is as neat
As a lark's shadow, that one grown
To a forbidding, dark domain;
Yet do we want some tower built,
Be it of moving, marching dust
Where soldiers tried, and failed, to make their thrust.

SONNET

Jordan that feeds from far Mount Hermon's snow,
Thames with its fogs and warehouses and docks,
Dargle whose alders dip on little rocks,
The Nile where heavily feluccas go,
Untroubled Avon in flat watermeadow
Or the mad pacing Rhine of many shocks,
Medway that swings the tackle through the blocks,
Deben now still, but for two boys who row;
The waters that will storm a city's gate
Or lie in glazing pools above a slope,
Or lessen, or become immoderate :
All these I feel within me and their scope
Carried by veins throughout my whole estate,
So quiet is my face and wild my hope.

ODYSSEUS DYING

I think Odysseus, as he dies, forgets
Which was Calypso, which Penelope,
Only remembering the wind that sets
Off Mimas, and how endlessly
His eyes were stung with brine;
Argos a puppy, leaping happily;
And his old Father digging round a vine.

Beat Drum, Beat Heart

1946

Part One

MEN IN WAR

Shouts rang up the street
War War it has come
Like leaves they were blown :
A spear from its corner
A summons on paper
Or buckle to thumb :

In the dark of a room
Old fears were known
By wrinkled up cheeks
And by young wives
Bent back at the waist
To kiss them alone :

But light were their feet
As thoughts were broken
And barriers thrown —
Out of copse out of brake
Out of field they were flown
To the tap of the drum.

*

Goodbye the milkcart pony
Standing in the sun;
The creaking basket
Of a baker's round;
And summer's garden besom
Sweeping on the ground
Then pausing; work unfinished
And work done.

Goodbye to the inn's warmth
Of views on beer and crop,
Where each man's talk
Is well known as his gait;
Goodbye to what the village
Knows and hears; to that late
Word at the lit door
Of a small shop.

Goodbye such emptiness
As loiters up and down
To show its friends
The new pup on a string,
Or with some tight-held flowers
Goes mutely visiting,
On Sundays, in the cleanness
Of a town.

*

All this is gone, a lost age,
Gust-torn like a picture page
That flutters, sidles down, then lies :
For a new sight now stings men's eyes
As, carried in a wind that sweeps
Them over shores and crags, — what steeps
They'll view, how take a city's height,
Where their force will next alight
Or like a spark will strike the sea,
Into what gates they bring a key —
Not one among the many knows.
But hopefully a trumpet echoes
Under arch of colonnade;
And shivering but unafraid
Others in pale air will roll
With bedding and with bamboo pole,
Plank cart and piebald pony,
Jerking over hills and *li*.
Look at them, at march or rest :

A gipsy walking gave the breast
To this one, and he likes to feel
Peril snapping at his heel;
While he, that Dublin bucko there,
At Liffey's edge who'd spit and swear,
Now whistles 'Killaloe' quite plain
Through the drenching Flemish rain;
Another, that in passing smiles
With pleasure at the red-curled tiles
Of homes; or he whose limbs are free,
Or knobbed like Kentish cobnut tree;
Pale Yorkshireman with eager gullet
And lank wrist — each one is yet
That god the Mexicans have sung
Who was in Paradise made young.
You will have heard some call them mad.
But whether any of them had
A doubt, which for a moment stood
Shy as roebuck in a wood
Before, startled, it fled in haste,
Is forgotten and effaced;
Or whether, to the night air
Extending patiently and where
Lyra throbs and Lynx spies
And Draco's coils anatomize,
They turned for help, with dry lips,
Pumping heart, wet fingertips
And gulping breath — historian
Or plaque will never say. All I can
Tell is, that as clouds which seem
Too soft may harden till they gleam
Like iron shields, then clash their scorn
Downward, by veined anger torn;
As fire through Leinster's bowels ranged;
Or as the French king's blood was changed
Who saw the Englishmen at Cressy;
As a pibroch's wail would free
Some heavy sword from off its strap
And give the plaid a tighter wrap;

As on a gentle morning, youths
To whom a lute, a rose, were truths,
Fought from thick-rigged galleass
With savagery that saved the Mass;
As those by nature wise and mild,
Twelve provinces of forest and wild
Rivers, terrors, ravines crossed
And mountains, half their number lost,
On the Long March which lasted three days
And a year : so war will braze
My metal. I declare, that with the oldest
Of our ills pressed on me, borne on me like
    A storm which no mere plan can shift
    Or strength dispel, with danger turned
From a low thunder rolling in the hills
To an immediate hurt, I am aware
    No time but now ever existed,
    This was I meant for, here I am man :
Which — before a fox saw villages
Die out when the Euphrates changed its bed,
    Or lazy air first woke to tower,
    Or hunters could hear northern winds,
While grasses whipped their legs, moan in the rocks —
Men learned, men knew, men felt, men understood.
    The fact is proved and clear, that war
    Rescinds what mattered, rends each form.
My hand, no longer casual and loose plucking
Under a filtering of trellised leaves,
    With careful and slight trigger act
    Gives vast effect; wishes once scattered,
Vague as any drift of gipsies, have now
Gathered from their road and ditch and plain
    Into one march of power; thoughts that were
    Finches starting from a thicket
Wing to where the eagle and the sun
Beat fiercely in a far and dazzled reach,
    High from the ground's indignity :
    Witness how David, rid of foes,
Grieves most; and Caesar sets up Pompey's statue;

Over Alps how emperors can boast
 In fight and Holy, then, be crowned.
 O praise events that led me to this
Fate, whose searchlight-cone, or glint on hilt
Points out the place where I can show my whole
 And candid self : let me be great,
 Bold, gilt by that esteem
Each lover longs for in a woman's eyes
To flood his soul with bliss and to uphold
 Supreme compulsion and desire
 With governance, salvation, succour,
Monstrous commands, and favour. Let me die :
Cut out my heart and hold it to the sun
 In fury; may its blood run slowly
 Under root and stone of time,
To rise in temples where ash-whitened Shiva,
The abhorred, renews by fire, and urge
 Crusaders in far massacre
 To tread the winepress of the Lord.

Brothers, this is our cloud, our hidden night.
We, being obscured ourselves, know nothing,
 In this darkness find no frame,
 No ladder to climb in clear air,
No tap or chip of bricks on a bright day;
But lean together as if chained to pillars,
 Under scourge from the whole world.
 And now not I, but at all cost
The other, must be saved from harm. Look how
In chaos they are carrying a boy
 On strong arms, with safe steps, or lifting
 In the half-drowned enemy,
Their names lost like a voice in the storm, shown
On the scroll of the sea, hushed in passages
 And space of air, of empty windy
 Air, or shouted by a noise
Uncurling to implacable explosion,
Then vanished, gone. Note how in this turmoil
 It is strange as myth to meet

A man who sows his land in calm,
A pigeon nest, joy of a watermill :
For in our blood we feel the heavy pace
     Of cataracts and, in our limbs,
     The tremor of small leaves that shake
Beside them, on their banks, perpetually.
We are a madness, shrill over the ground,
     We are the bass notes' melancholy;
     We are the men who pulled Lorca
Between arches by tall-shadowed houses;
We are a man dragged and killed on the outskirts
     Of a town in Spain. We know both
     Chill and warmth of the guerrillas
Lumbering through snow, defending Moscow;
The shelterwarden's knack of seeming mild,
     His inner rage. Another time,
     Close under the soil we go
In trenches, huddled in a reek of furs,
Like pictures in a bestiary : for cunning,
     Fellowship and cruelty
     Live in my palms and shins and back;
And glitter-eyed, like flocks at night, are those
Who camp in dips and hollows of a field.
     Each thing that stirs, warily
     Is watched and feared and felt and spied,
And silence, or the din of gunfire, guessed
For signs. Sappers have kneeled; they tap and wait
     And listen for the faint of sounds,
     Then know their fate. O smile O cry
For minutes hang on rumours of a rumour,
Hours fall to a wreck, and seconds beat
     As in Cassandra's pulsing neck
     With my defeat or with your doom,
With answer to our two encountered ranks,
With hurts, much longing, sickness and huge dread.

But look, how this one's glad and how he grips
His steel; nothing astounds and all is safe,

Lightfooted, as once in a lad
Angel led and dog at heel.
With talent for his pith, fame in his eye,
He makes design and chance, by strength of touch,
Agree like music on the map
Of high campaign towards his end.
Then will the Incas blaze near to, like suns.
Rochelle unbend itself. Madrid give in.
A prodigy. But in the haste,
And in the clamour and the sweat,
This sharp acclaim is his own shout, the ray's
Behind his blink of tears : he cannot tell
That over waste the dawn spilled out,
The street abandoned when he came.
But I — what I have done has come untied
In spite of all I've tried or said. For long
I fail. I can do nothing right,
But heap mistake upon mistakes;
While war's old cart goes slowly creaking on
Into the disillusionary years
Of its real destiny, where later
My own enemy will tread.
Where is my cause, that seems as cold as a blown
Mist? It was so firm, so solid. Must I think
It's I have grown into a ghost?
All is reversed; all is astray;
And reason an old mirror full of flaws.
Gestures that were heroic are remote
As black clouds in a battle-piece;
But they need rain in Barcelona
Where there's blood up to the second storeys.
God of hopes, how you misguide us. We,
Who thought we had the heart and sinews
Of strong beasts, of noble birds —
Head high the running stag, the great in pinion —
Find we emboss, with virtues and with oath,
Only a blason, stony cut,
And which the weathers chip and winds
Chafe. I'd said our coats would boast our pride —

But see, mine's foul and ragged with deceit
  Because, by Ronda bridge across
  The double cliffs that sheer to drop eight
Hundred feet, and from whose rocks so many
Pigeons flew, instead, the violated
  Nuns fall, fluttering.
  We thought, this is warm, this is different,
This abscinds us from all past fights, as we marched among
      haycocks
With some of the brambles ripe, but the same chill
  Lies on our hair, as in pale winter
  When the saplings are cut through.
Indeed, there's more of torture; and the crime
Of children with their peace hurled into air :
  More fault, more insult and more shame
  Than can be cleaned out from our core —
Unless Time, in its passage round the world,
Should, like an idle workman, make a halt.

                          *

  When Jacob laid his head upon a stone,
  Jacob of Aldgate, he was now alone
  In the dear land of Judah. Here the guns
  All day had uttered threats like benisons
  Over a ground where love and sorrow erred,
  As had the prophets that his father heard.
  Here there was woe, here desolation came
  Advancing long ago, showing her name
  Nettles and saltpits and the voice of birds
  In empty window-frames : and still could words
  Of mercy, loving kindness, goodness that must
  Come, quiver in whiteness like hill dust,
  To fade at night time, while through bushes ranged
  The small sheep, restless, with their herds, unchanged.
  All else is silent. As he turns on rocks
  And olive roots, his memory unlocks
  Some Reader chanting in a quiet stressed
  By pages turned together as a forest

Quickly stirs its leaves; the careful tread
Of carrying the crimson velveted,
The red-wrapped Torah, through a muttered dark
Of men more shy and inward than the Ark;
Or, near the Minories, the hint and fact
Of what man's wits can seize, know, make, transact;
A sale bill of old stock-in-trade across
A dirty shop front; and the grey hurry; gloss
Of rain on pavements; and each market friend
Who stood and argued, argued without end.
These are the last good things he will have known.
For should he live or die, all's twisted and grown
Monstrous from this force of arms; a force
Allowing as much refuge and recourse
As there was bastion or parapet
Against the treachery on Olivet;
A force more harmful than sore ages spent
Burdened by common ache of punishment;
Bringing no gain, nothing redeemable : instead
Blackness and rubble lying over Samson dead.

*

'I was a Greek. I climbed Aornos' rock for Alexander.
My foot slipped on the pine needles and my breath hurt.
Round me men hurtled down to where the Indus
Washes that great crag.'

　　　O men O commanders

'I lived by the Border. Mist would bead our woollen cloaks,
Our pelts and faces, on the mornings when we woke
Ready for foraying. I died in the grass
As lonely as a crow.'

　　　O men O commanders

'From Hejaz I. Much I endured of thirst and of sore eyes.
I rode for one who led us and for gain, and knew
The camel-thorn, the clefts, the stinging wind
Of promises unkept.'

   O men O commanders

'I was a Catalan. I fought in hills near Teruel.
I was so cold and hungry. Who was foe or brother
No one learnt. Black mounds under the snow
Were bodies or else earth.'

   O men O commanders

'I a Venetian whom the Genoese strewed on deep water.
Spars and oars of all our fleet had snapped like reeds.
I drowned, thinking of young fishermen
Who wade in a lagoon.'

   O men O commanders

       *

'Here is his picture; you can't see the smile.'
The line of the nose is sad, and the mouth.
'This silver frame is all his monument.'
He looks astonished. That one
Has lowered eyes, as if he knew.

'Sir, the patient has no face, and hears
Nothing.' But the small fitful noise
Of a hill wind is in his ears.

'They must have drifted many
Weeks before they lost hope;
Their bodies had no disfiguring marks
Of oil or sores, but were frayed and bleached
Like an old rope.'

       *

Seeing great
Warriors in my head,
And how each yields
His breath in state :
Aruns with mouth against Etruscan asphodel;
The small waves, steeled and glittering,
Of Pompey caught in the shallows;
That stab to Brian, the old king;
Beloved Sir John Chandos on the field
In Vienne, whom the avenging,
Fighting knights can hallow —
I let out my sap,
With sobs, near rotted
Mangold roots that smell
As sour as failure.

*

Stumbling in retreat,
  The others, still with armed pack,
  Feel flints cut into their feet,
  Rage at cobbles, curse their knees,
  Thinking they'd been fools to fight.
All's wrecked on either hand.
  We can never talk
  To others : who would understand?
The sight
  Of plough up-ended, spoiled rick,
  Scarecrow in a torn field,
  Is fellow to this fanatic
  Whose staring eyes and rigid walk
  Keep by me like some dented shield.
How strange, these gables over us and roofs
  In blackness where
  The rain pours from the guttering,
  This splashed filthiness of hoofs.
Cards lie scattered in a tomb.
  Someone picks them up and sees
  Instead of Queen and Jack,

[33]

Hector, Judith and *Lahire,*
Lancelot, Alexandre,
Who should have never left the womb.
French. Throw 'em back.
We hid, we ran, we had
    To reach the water; then
    Our oars dipped in to make
    Eyeless sockets of a crone.
For heaven's sake,
    How soon will I be let alone?
Past the thin trees of France,
    Or in a wicked wind from side-streets,
    Trail a rifle, drag your lance.
Dawn comes up grey and meets
    A woman smiling at us, mad;
    She puts a finger to her lips,
    Shakes her head and slips
    Down an alley.
Night will find the bare plain
    We captured; there we crawl and press
    Through dead ruins of our pain.
My mind's root is bruised : all
    I need is nullness
    And to lie where I fall.
Everything will be so changed,
    I'll feel a clown, the cog
    Will never fit, I'll be estranged,
    Fears this stalwart who upheld
    Enormous courage
    In monotony more wasteful
    And more weighty than steel wreckage,
    And as vacant as the air
    Round jealous soldiers' arguments.
A voice has yelled :
    Oh God, I dreamt I was where
    Women washed our bloodied garments
    Out, and looked at us through leafy,
    Latticed windows, and were sorry
    For us, endlessly sorry.

The last one,
   Trudging by his side, is thinking
   Of his grizzled dog
   At home, with ears aback, blinking,
   Old and happy in the sun.

*

By any men who ever hung on trees
Or who were left, strung over wire,
To turn their heads now this way and now that,
Mire to their knees or groin; and by
The sour weeds on a father's grave;
By nettles grown near outworks of a fort;
By a church buttress which the hurt were laid
Against, their plaints heavy and broken
Like stone draperies of saints —
Never, never again.

By the square, tragic mouth
Of wrath, that may be shameful, hapless,
Or degraded by disaster; and by
Murder done in clean air
And truth wrung out as if a dirty cloth;
By everyone who carried in his mind
Some bright image like a coin,
Yet could not give small change
Or find a right retort, surprised
And piteously;

By any homeless ones who sit,
Emptied of feeling, on a heap of bricks
And grit which was their all;
And chiefly by those who cannot sleep
But — fretting like the wind at night —
Think ceaselessly, had they advanced,
Gone back, been forthright, or declared themselves
Some other time, or place, or way, there would
Have been no utter, endless grief : I swear,
I pray, never again.

[35]

Part Two

MEN AT PEACE

Mist has fallen quietly on air
That once stirred past a mountain fighter's head,
And silent are the rushes where
A boy into Scamander bled.
Hidden in the ground are bane
And warring; and the bitter groans
And orders and the leader's tread
Forgotten in the long rain,
Like little birds that hop among the stones
Of Hebrides and all lapsed islands.

       'Under the alders
       Just let me be;
       All there is here
       Is drip from alders
       Into a lake
       Of half sunk logs.'

How heavily white fogs
Will roll through fields of memory
To cover pain with northern balm.
Even this Southerner can seldom speak,
Now war is done but, sitting
In his courtyard, listens to the creak
Of chestnut boughs. Only a leaf will make
A shadow on his wall; the sun
And no one else, can overtake
Thoughts which are too slowly spun
To snare the reason for each hour
Of living, or to understand
Why the clock shows in the tower,
Why the blood beats in his hand.

'From bed, I hear
Them sweep the morning's
Echoing street,
While the aged maid
Comes in to set
The washing ewer
On a chair.'

Somewhere in a field, there's short grass growing.
With an ear to it, one almost feels
The blades spring. The mind is prone
Or supine, and as calm
As this poor bit of ground
That carries signs of donkey-grazing
And the smells of summer, and that's bound
By a wall so loose and easy-built
That much of it has fallen. Weals
Of many hundred seasons lie
In smallest bract of humble weed or bloom.
But all at once, senses and vision tilt
In shock to the stupendous sky,
Then down, to wonder — could this be the stone
That was once rolled back from a tomb?

'O who can bear
The brass and yells
That shiver through
The mended village, while they
Shoulder flags; it grates
Against the teeth :
A blizzard in
An east wind.'

Aeneas carried an oar inland,
Knowing the broken coast and pirate ships,
And where they asked him, What's that tool?
He thought it right for a new town to stand;
And as a bird inside a wicker cage,
Kept from all hawking doubt, uncertain rage
Of things, will stretch its feathers to their tips —

So vines may bud; and mirrors fill
With movement; after a trampling from a fool,
Spiders again may sling their webs in dew;
And a rock's outcrop on a hill
Be taken up and cut, as men devise,
For arches to enclose some lengthening view;
While from the lazy meadows spires will rise.

     'Ted's father, leave
     The graveyard beside the canal;
     Put cap to head
     As you wipe your eyes
     With the back of your hand.
     And you, leave the memorial
     In the dark vault.
     No love dies ever,
     And no fault.'

Free from hateful foreigners —
The way they cut their hair or clear their throat
Or dig their elbows in one's private ribs — each
Is back into his old coat
And usage, land and life :
'Now we can own ourselves, like decent folk.'
In Wales, racked by rivers
Silvering dark lore with rapid speech;
In the scant North, whose men and trees
Make strong and thrifty growth; in Suffolk, flat
As mud, where the slow-voiced have ever spat
From barges beating into estuaries;
Everywhere, builders and their jobs in life
Can jogtrot on again like husband and wife.

     'Contentment's when
     An ache has cleared
     And left us whole,
     While from the borough benches
     Ringing can be heard :

And Lateran
Or Lutheran,
The dear clang
Breaks into the soul.'

The sea has brought her dowry, and the tide
Has laid its jetsam all along the shore.
But up the hill there's cordial
And beer, new curtains, ashtrays that were coral
Found in a far gulf, and relatives
Crushed closely, joking, to admire the bride :
She will be shrewd and practical, and a just
Comfort to this fisherman who must
Tomorrow drag his trawler-nets once more
In rain, on the sea bed. The sunset gives
The guests, on leaving, music played
Along the crowded esplanade.
And later, a law-copier who lives
On deeds in unstopped verbiage,
Thinks of a past Regatta week,
Rest, and the ferry's shriek,
And sees the crawling wave upon the page.

'How civil to dispute
In neutral air
Of judges' courts, dusty
As a sawmill where
The churning wheel outside
Clanks in the same place to chide
Whoever cannot make, assemble,
Drive and gear together
Lasting, hard repute.'

*

But here's a morning walked alone
    By someone who, at worst, has known
    Work inside a tutor's book,
    And care, in dry or troutless brook.

[39]

Past glinting bracken of midday
Where only flies and midges play,
Past a stone wall, past furzes mean,
Past a straggle of boreen
With dusty burrs and beechtree mast
And fine fir needles on it cast,
Past tumbling plaint of notes that stop
Him dead to listen, up at top,
Past tufted bog, and past the baulk
Of sloe hedge and wet bramble stalk
He goes, to feel the hours that lag
Beside him, run to the fore and drag
His wishes into being filled
With wilds to alter, forms to build.
Soon drafts and invoices are stirred
　By the numbed hands of agents in furred
　Hats, or else by ledger clerks
　Quick-tempered in the heat where barques
　Ride and part the harbour scum
　Outside; till vessels lately come
　From Naples or the Baltic Sea
　Lean against a Dublin quay
　And from their holds pitch out large crates
　Of statuary, railings, gates,
　Amazon and warrior,
　Head of pagan empress, or
　Apollo with his sun's horns
　That workmen think their Saviour's thorns.
Then for planks and platforms fit
　To roll those pedestals of granite
　Quarried in his own hills
　In which the wind cries out and chills
　The nesting plovers of Glencree;
　For all must shape as perfectly
　As this well-reasoned rockery
　Of mosses over grotto's eye
　Where, unseen, a trickle learns
　Darkness through the dripping ferns.

Ending a path, how curious
These figures of fierce Eolus:
Like two great metal men, they blow
Their curving streams to merge and flow
Cross-rippled in a bowl; while out
Of a snub dolphin nose, or spout
Of lips, more veils of water jet
To fall in tiers, and then beset
Slippery shoulders and the charms
Of nymphs with shells and clutching arms.
Now all's finished, placed and still:
Nothing base and nothing shrill.
Here, stone shadows of a cup
To griffin heads are fluted up;
Here, acanthus leaves and horn
Of rams, on urns of bronze are borne;
Here, in sunk gardens, gods could sip
At this huge tazza's marble lip;
While here, the mounting grass succeeds
Terrace by terrace, till it leads
To pebbled slopes in black and white
That imitate each turn and flight
Where mules go steeply up and down
And laden, in an Umbrian town:
Through all, could no more come regret
Than wild hare with her leveret.
And so, by reed and lake, where the twin
Horses prance in discipline
As, delicate of nose and leg,
They wing the air and seem to beg
Such loveliness to stay, by length
Of alley in the sun's strength,
By each invention and device
That tames the mountains at a price,
You'll wander, and by flickered shade
Of statues in a beech glade,
To let your inmost sadness fall
Blackly, under ilex pall.

*

So will a voice at random
In the fields become
A structure of compassionate sounds
Which you will climb like ladders in the air,
Until the mighty fugal arguments declare
You noble, sad and great.

So, in a Gothic window,
Virtue with all force must press
In power. Unquenched, the embers glow
Round Peter's robe that's greener than sea deeps;
Saint Eustace aims his shaft as the stag leaps
Through the Cathedral darkness and the dread.

So, if a Londoner,
You go from Amen Corner
Into Paul's, on up under the dome's
Vast hum of silence where the many tongues are tomes :
You sit among first books, and read, if you deserve,
Of *Troilus and Criseyde*, how the pen stabs with goodness
And undoes the nerve.

So someone will detect
And map proportions that connect
New threads of reasoning and light
Moving unceasingly in growth, or in the sea's
Suspense, in stars that comb the air with tracks
And problems as with parallax.

So the lens grinder, blest in name, in soul,
In understanding of our load
Of human plight,
And for defining attribute and mode
Of God into one luminous, transparent whole,
Stays gentle and upright.

*

Such fruit, clamped to the wall,
Fills us till we're gorged,
Or till the rags tear
Or brads bend.
Have we by chance used
Nails the tinkers forged?

*

For look, philosophers have lungs
That choke on glass-grit, it's been proved;
And children scream; and old men steal,
Or die of cancerous tongues;
We dip slow oars of thought into the night
And find we have not moved;
And what are libraries? Can printed page,
Or even hassock and cold
Stone smelling of piety, assuage
My inner tide of doubt? Light
Is dimmed, the scene rolled,
Smallish dust blows from the stage;
And the dance of a young teague
With casual-cunning toe and heel
Becomes a ponderous Germanic gigue;
And where, by twisted fountain and by ways
So devious and delighting that the running gaze
Was lost, enchanted, in the sight — yet
The very stillness of the air's a fret,
A hint, a whisper of the growing
Need for some harsh harrowing.

*

A room where arguing intellectuals whine,
Then limply give their hand and start again;
Another, where the Adam-style pilasters
Echo with the self-important cough
Of old and knuckle-rubbing men who like
The softly lapping fire, the rustled *Times*,

After a hard day's hunting : those who once
Had felt at home in either, are aghast.

We'll go no more to the woods, they're now bricked up
And villas grow as campion by the way;
And all along wet tarmac hoardings show
In boredom, like the new and cleanly pub;
And a mock Tudor tea-house mocks itself,
Mocks hunger, and the fools who think that beams
And pewter jugs and cakes are carrying
Them daintily into a turbid past.

We'll walk instead on pavings and on paths
Where grass is trodden and the elms are doomed,
And dogs, the smart-trimmed and the common dogs,
Play in the Parks, and small boys pitch their stumps,
And tramps unwrap things from a newspaper,
And women mince, and prams are wheeled along
For ever, under careless sweeping clouds
To the far roar of buses round about;

Or, from a City roof, we'll see how soot
Lies in the flowerpot left on a sill;
How iron rusts; and the eroded bricks
Rise up in grimy insult to the air,
Whichever way they're set; and humans live
As bindweed grows over a clinkered mound —
Here, and at back of equal towns whose streets
Such windows scan, while never a face looks out.

For now our thoughts are caught in thicket growth
Which slowly strangles them with age; they feel
Mute as the woollen horns, fixed as the chase
In darkened forests of some tapestry
Which has been stared at, for no purpose, for
Too long; being as stale and as exhausted
As the parlour walls, and yellow air,
And ticking clock, of all dead afternoons.

[44]

We have turned back from Tragedy, that land
Of warning and of storms and godlike speech
Upbraiding us, griping our mind and marrow,
As in winter, trunks of trees seem twisted
One way by a giant's hand — gone back
To comic papers, and euonymus,
The promenade, and sandfleas on the beach,
And strum and tinkle of the blackface coons.

Once, in the dark of obsequies, our passion
Thickened till it grew to total might;
And once in childhood, over the wall : and there
The river's shining promise in the meads;
But now, as salesmen moving through half lights,
We might be women, tired out, endlessly traipsing
Rainy suburbs, on uneven heels,
In ugliness, unkindness and in waste.

Meanwhile, through institutions towering
Like their unending, shadowless grey days,
There's been amassed in record, ledger, file
And down long office corridors of fact,
Index and tabulation of our deeds,
So that all things are noted and exact,
Balanced, budgeted and accounted for —
Except that life seems pointless and disgraced.

*

By all ruined learning,
Where it may be :
By saint that spoke
On small isle's space
Whose silverweed
Now meets the sea;
And Glendalough
Where oar's stroke
Guides the tripper
Through deep rest

[45]

And quiet face
Of hermit's creed;
By systems of grace;
The good in all things
Confused as talk,
Or stray as goats
In cemetery
Of Muslim bones;
And Peter's pence
Crammed in a case;
Or Jews caught
In the Law's decay,
Who push their prayers
In cracks of stones
At the Temple's base;
By Christ so crippled
From what's been taught,
He calls for a crutch
And tries to walk;
And by each empty
Site in the heart
Once great, yes,
As Armageddon
Was when manned
And walled apart,
But stared at, now,
Quite openly —
I know how much
Has fallen, how
Akhnaton's mildness
Slid like sand. . . .

Oh, lights are showing
In Guildford, and people
Are yawning for tea.

*

Whoever is in low
Relief, faintly embossed,
Take heed, take care,
For you will be erased.
No more is noon when the groom shaves,
Peace under trees, or safety
The gilt vanes of Penshurst
In the sun. But time
And place are strewn
With cloud, lost like fumes
Within a darkness fit
For burning rubbish,
And the knife's release :
It lops what's done
To let new growth swell out.
O that I'd bud and break
And truly live — for look,
What heroes make us proud :
Such as refuse, deny,
And with perverted strength
Draw back, or those
Who most abundantly
And warmly breathe, and use
Their love, and swear, and fight
Into the press of things?
Find me a cause
Or a catastrophe
To crack and shake the false,
The phrased, the laggard pleas
Of a restraining clause.
For now, thank God, no more
Dismayed by Death —
(I blushed to think of her,
Froze in the night, and held
My breath) — I'll fondly give
My seamless skin and know her,
Like a man.

[47]

Part Three

Clearly as a fife and drum
   Down the village lane may come,
   As bells may suddenly be hurled,
   Or willow and the ash be swept
   Into greying gusts of fear,
   As it rains, as starts the wren
   Or suddenly a maiden wept :
   So is caring ever near,
   Ever hidden.
           We
   Who watch a woodman split a tree
   To its pale heart, at any breath
   May feel love with one heavy blow
   Cleaving us from head to toe.
   Then life and the whole sky turn chill
   And set us shivering, as when
   Europa, with her friends at play
   In hot sweet sultry fields, away
   By the great creamy bull was led
   Along a bitter shore, until
   Her hair was lifted by the wind
   And over the dark ripples sped
   The two to rough-topped Crete.

Even the ageing, the wise-eyed,
   The disenchanted women; those
   Most unassailable whose prose
   Of peace is round them like a dress;
   Even the unforgetting ones
   Who'd let no further pain compress
   Their lives; and those whose memory
   Is faded like a token saved —
   (That letter or that strand of hair
   Which has lost all its power and sense;

As, on a wall, a sword can hang
Quite disregarded, yet engraved
With battle honours of the past,
And rust eats out what was immense) —
They'll feel its touch; and those who've tried
To act like vagabonds dispersed
In public gardens, through May's hush
Will find the dark red hawthorn flush
And warmth, will know the pang and fear
Of couples that year after year
Shelter beneath it, stand in thrall
Without a word, and wait for the first
Thunder drops to fall.

Exalt this giant cloud, this clash,
   This storm that shakes our inmost being,
   Cracks foundations, and discovers —
   In the instant of a flash —
That what was old is fresh and strange;
Exalt the boldness and delight
Of finding that if in our lover's
Eyes we stare, on shafts of light
Like will, like sight, like air we range
To every landscape of the feelings,
   Every climate of the temper :
   To an innocence of mornings
   Milky new, without a name;
Or among dust and tracks that bring
Us nearer to some ancient fame;
Or to the icy wind and mountain;
To hard deserts of a plain
Where monks, in emptiness of heat,
On rocks rasp their hems and feet;
To the wild places; or to ease
Of rivers; or contemptuous seas :
   In turbulence and risk.

For watch : wherever someone grieves,
   As on a terrace along which
   Scatter and skelter the dry leaves;

Or on a foggy waterfront;
In shops; or in the City square
Whose starlings clatter by the thousand
While at open windows, working
Typists fill the answering air;
In every time and place and land
(Perhaps they've known the other stress
Of stoical foolhardiness,
But this time without heaume or casque,
Sallet or helmet, as in war
Their men — and they — had worn before)
Do women, unremarked, alone,
Stroking their forearm absently,
Or most composed and easy, ask
Only for the might, the nerve
To love (for God's sake don't be grateful),
To agree, give tribute, serve,
Perish, and bear the brunt.

*

Where is the lumber-room of what was important?
The bric-a-brac of old feelings? Finished, put away.
And where the motes of ideas we breathed for our *now*?
Lost corridors, stray paths in the woods to our *here*?
Forgotten, of no account. In me, I feel
New space, new time, strangely careened and on whose
Axes spin my world, as you and I —
The man, the woman — tremble face to face.
The air is filled with power, hesitancy,
And awareness sharp as a blade's edge :
The lightest gesture, the least sign, can alter
Our whole fate. Opposed like this, we know,
We two, the other's soul is the most threatening
And immediate fact there's ever been —
You are so whole and real, he says, and keeps
Back tears; she, Nothing can stop the force
Of this great hour. I, as a woman, know
That from this confrontation such momentous

Grace or plight will come, it is the reason
I was born peasant in the rain
Or one who trails her mantle in the hall;
That centuries have waited and prepared —
Rehearsing with mimed passion and mock battles —
For this one and overpowering cause :
A cause whose glare lights up the skies and roofs,
Streets, spires, alleys of the mind
With an intensity so sacrificial
That its blazing flash and burning shadow
Fill with unseen, heroic acts. What
Can profane, he thinks, such faith as this? And she :
In finding you, I find myself, will cry.

For now I understand all twofold things;
How dark and light, matter and spirit, gut
And brain can be acquainted, how they accord :
Angel and beast in me are one : because
The midway heart is held between
What's private, base, and what's diffused and rare,
Binding the two as the sun's power can weld
The soil, where his foot rests, into quick life
With upper levels of the air. Through me
All contraries of grief and joy are strung :
I am rage and mercy, impulse and slow patience,
Folly and wisdom; I am the rain-filled wind,
The blade that suffers drought. I've tolled
A bell of duty harshly; groaned and wept
For mercy like a saint on a stone floor.
One fears me, and of one I go in terror;
I am those Fates with scant hair and red eyes
And brittle bones, who so disdain the young;
I am the thread that stretches to be nicked.
I am a parody and extreme, but round me
All natural things are stupid, without substance :
People with idiot faces, in nameless houses,
Going on errands that can have no meaning.
Aloof from others, I still speak for them
And must fulfil them. Bending my ear to catch

The oracle, at the same time it's I,
Fume-crazy croaking sibyl, who predict it.

In full process, now, of secret planning,
Anguish and boredom — and again anguish, all the time
Feeling his presence and voice : at night when all's quiet,
During the racking day, but chiefly in crowds
Where I always think I have found him, or see someone like
        him —
Each faculty and each nerve (for he tests me in every
Thing at all moments), each vigour is taut, alert,
Made into a halter for triumph which now almost gentles
Up to my hand and then, will slip away;
Each fibre throughout my frame is used, with enough
Force and guile to wrench away an empire,
Or to exhaust the world with strategies.

*

Should anyone ask, Where are these battlefields?
Perhaps in the country house
Where a clammy mist falls over the garden,
Fills muddied lanes
And surges into the guest room.

Perhaps in some Park.
Municipal ducks, freezing lake,
Reeds like straw,
And an old bottle caught in the ice.

Perhaps by sand near prickled,
Sea-pitted coral rocks,
Where fond hope and insufficiency
Are the same as anywhere else;
While in the heat
Roads blind you with whiteness.

These are my Flanders, Valley Forge, Carthage.

*

Principles are my breath,
They fly like vapour from my mouth :
O I am mad, mad
As whorls of air round hills, chilled
By shining mountains before
Tumbling to warm itself over
The breast of plains; turning
In branches of the carob tree,
Then seeking shade and grace
Under a marble bridge, a causeway;
As harlot water
Feeling, always moving, among
Palaces whose stone has
Stepped its weight into my arms.
My breathing is the raucous
Laughter and the clatter from
A Venetian supper-tent
Whose awning stripes billow to noise
And negro-carried wine;
Untamed exuberance of limbs
Shaken by voodoo Erzulie;
Thickness of tropic
Fire from scarlet flowers
Whose leaves creep and thrust
And spike and choke each others' lives —
This air inspires me now.

*

I said inspired : fully
    I mean it. Each word,
Each event, shows me its own,
    Natural tact;
From chance, or proper command,
    I am the elect.
My devotion is felt as it walks
    Beside the young preacher
Who once climbed up to the pulpit,
    A rose in his mouth —

And look how confidence
   Can lie in my hand
That's loose and open, power
   Along my arm
Smoother than lip of a shell;
   And how my gladness
Breaks the sea in spurts
   Of dolphin foam.
How easy to move, to act!
   Forebodings have fled
As bat-form shreds of cloud
   Escape at sunrise;
What was difficult
   Is plain as noonday
Heat in light that dazzles
   The lost marshes
Over which our thoughts
   Shake in the air
Like larks : this light, strong
   As was the vision
That Aquinas saw
   And then fell silent
To dispute no more, —
   Giving us glory,
Lustre, unity, —
   Wakens the Future
From half-lidded sleep :
   Who, with his eyes
Near blinded by behests
   And glare, shuts them,
Deciding to impose
   The shadow of old
Doubts, policies,
   And debts again.

Within our curtained alcove
   We are so near
To stab each other : deeps
   Of uncertainty

Must hang between our heads.
  My destiny,
And yours, swing up and down
  In scales that give
No justice, only judgment;
  While we watch
Grave statements rise like dust
  Of war, havoc
From messages that stray,
  Fears from a freshly
Toppled plan; and then
  Observe disjunction,
Incoherence, lack
  Of sense : with pity
And the ancients' terror
  On our face.

*

'As through the field
Walked I and my true lover,
I did discover
Goodness in gateways heeled
By cattle, dreams in the meres
And hope in taste of clover.
Now all I need
Is to forget,
For since our quarrel
All in the world's a weed,
And tears are salt as sorrel.'

*

That slightest shiver of wind
  Before dawn is the shock
To my soul when it learns he has ceased,
  Yes, ceased, to care.
Which blunder have I made,
  Where was I wrong,

To be shown that miracles
    Are past? What
Have I done, for retribution
    To come on me swiftly,
Savagely and teach me
    That fortitude
Is no use and cannot prevent
    My being destroyed?
'Pourrvou que cela dourre . . .'
    Had said a mother,
Bending to blow her nose
    In the Corsican gutter.

I bit into the day
    To find it rotten;
Would I could spit it out.
    Recriminations,
Bitterness, reproach,
    Have opened a gulf,
Have cracked Time in two —
    Time that in splendour
Of success elided
    Into long
Negations of itself;
    Time that could be
Timeless, without front,
    Without direction,
Pace or guidance; mixed
    Until those Persian
Arrows blackening
    The sun, and children
Who feared dusk, were one;
    A Time fed
By many equal founts,
    So that the chirp
And clink and chattering
    Of Spring was twin
To shrivelled sycamore
    And the wet leaf

Of amber-dropping lime.
　　But now, sharpest
Calamity has cut
　　Its marks all round me :
Painful and precise,
　　Their steps and minutes
Cleave and allocate.

*

　　It's thought the Angel
Said to the first woman :
　　'Now, walk slowly
From the garden, slowly,
　　For perhaps
You will be called back.'
　　But God has despised me,
I am no longer watched,
　　My thoughts guessed,
Giving anxiety, care,
　　Giving alarm :
But ignored. This is defeat
　　Unalterable,
This is the worst, the most
　　Unrelenting revenge.

*

The wet wind storms the branches
And trees shake; the same wind,
　　Blowing where there are boats,
Jumps them against the mooring ropes.
　　Unless the tree uproots,
Or the rope breaks, or I go mad,
　　There is no leaving. When
I see him who has this contempt of me,
　　I feel a hot wave of sickness
Then quickly, cold despair. I think

[57]

How surely and easily
Could I have still held my advantage,
    Had I said this or done that;
And dreams recur, showing some new
    And splendid mastery
To give my pride a triumph in daylight,
    Instead of it cringing, begging,
Along tenebrous streets of the mind
    Where arch and girder are broken
And behind the dignity, degradation is seen,
    And stupidity, emptiness.
The friends of bereaved cities feel shame
    To look at them, they find nothing
Noble or great in devastation
    Of what was once entire.

                    *

She ran from the vast house and her pheasant-shooting
    brothers
Towards the light there was in learning, towards living.
Amused, eccentric, kind; a witty ghost, warm soul
And mighty to understand, slowly she'd speak or move
Or give her arm and look into the eyes of those
Entranced by her, to find (so her whole life, she hoped)
The superb effulgence, the total intimacy of two
Feeling minds. Most of them mocked her afterwards.
She was heroic. She died alone in herself as always.
The London pigeons wheeling in wind and traffic, the
    pressure
And pressmen at the church door, or inside : she was no-
    where in this.

A second one's young, and as she's walking down the street
Whose windows all of them have ferns in brass pots
And elderly ladies at desks answering their letters,
Her swimming eyes are remembering collegiate leaves.
She can discern no raddled cheeks, no sagging body
Of some collapsed Fury, no terror through her calm,

As she passes these victims of double dealing, or of powerful
Respectability, these reprobates and bullies, examples
Of bores, or what is raffish, pompous or calculating.
She thinks the worst her dreams can ever do to her
Is fail to show a mask of leaves, a crumbled urn.

A third one sees her tended, heavy-scented garden
From the verandah. A dog yawns. A cage swings.
Not a blister of paint, not a spiderweb, not a branch out of
    trim,
Not a blemish on a waxed table, not a dab of dirt in the
    kitchen —
And yet, under this bland and meticulous order, the blister,
The shaking thread, the imbalance, the blame, the horror are
    hidden
But always in mind. It's fifty years since there was a man
Who strolled and whistled, quick and carefree, like the
    whipping waves,
Whom she would have gone with, now as then, anywhere —
To a strange land with the wind rattling the window panes.
'Come on, dogs; well, little bird?' and her hand trembles.

*

               I can see
               Berenice dragging her robe
               Between bare pillars
               From the sun;
               Heloise a nun
               Still unconsolable;
               Kind Dorothy enduring
               Mist and rocks
               Colder than those of Cumberland;
               And Mary sweet as phlox;
               While Harriet has a scent
               Of water's edge
               Where now the pert
               And nervous mallard and teal
               Are watched by Parkgoers
               From a gravelled ledge

[59]

In air that's brisk and fluent.
But for my loss of heart,
My pain,
There's a tapping
Window blind, or
A muddle of rain.

*

Let me slip away or sleep
  Or die. How can I go back
  Into each day's
  Queasy remembering?

I envy the very old
  With their faces wiped clean
  Of moods and movement;
  No pulpy flesh under the skin :
  Only a covering for the skull.

Women who are silent in manner,
  Or wildly frivolous, or crazy,
  Or dispirited, or merely aimless
  And vague — do I seem one of them?

The ravaging
  Use of feeling and valour;
  All the uncommon goodness
  That's been spent,
  Laid waste.

Look at the tattered room
  Exposed to the sky.
  No splendour in this ruin,
  But shame in small wallpaper
  For all eyes.

The mind is open,
  Desolate, swinging in the wind
  Like a knocking gate;
  While autumn woods all smoulder
  Till put out by rain,
  And pigeons clip the empty air.

                    *

There's nothing
For an edifice. Not even
Such small figurines of clay
As are found in a tomb on the hillside :
Children, shawled and capped,
Carrying sheaves and dancing.
No weight is left, no tenderness,
As on a sarcophagus lid
Where man and wife lie knee to knee,
His bracelet twining on her wrist,
His marble fingers
Curving round her arm.

                    *

  By our crawling
  Spaniel-race;
  The lash of our remorse;
  By brutish things : snouts
  Grunting at Circe;
  Gaze of wrong
  From mottled venom-face;

  By the stretched tendons
  Of the two robbers;
  By him who thanked
  Or scolded each person
  More deeply than soul
  Ever since or before;

By the women who stood
Beside those nailed planks —
We who spoke low
Under our hoods —
For pity's sake, no more.

Part Four

WOMEN AT PEACE

Round my whole mind, the same
And snowy landscape lies
That once came with its blank
On Tobit's worried eyes
And gently covered up
His troubles. Earth is sealed.
Dead still the staring-coated
Bullocks in the field.
Stiff is each reed, each twig
Unmoved, each trickle stopped,
Unuttering, and seized
With numbness where it dropped.
Level and like all things,
Which way I turn my head,
With only a hunched bird
To show there's roof or shed
In country as well known
To me as home. But should
The scene thaw out, and I
Then wander by a wood
Or undergrowth of coppice
Fenced with ash, by farms set
Tightly in the weald,
By empty branches' net —

Still will the leaden road,
The sky, the death of sound,
The slaty cold and dumbness
Keep my senses bound
As in a trance — until
One morning when I wake,
Wake suddenly, not knowing
How, not knowing why,
Feeling a change to climates
Nearer South . . .

                    *

    Clear, clear
Like a young cockerel's cry,
The singing of a boy
Along a hill.
    I listen,
Free as this easy air
So thin, so clean.

    In the dark grove
Of mandarini trees
Under my window,
Snicking clacking gardeners
Take up the snatch of tune :
They curl it, turn it
And repeat it till it's twisted
Like the under-branches
They are cutting.
After that,
A little raking.

    No more
To be watched
By high and hungry gods,
But to feel light, drained;
To move about as I wish;
To get beyond this garden
To the wild slope.

                    [63]

Lying in its grass,
All I can hear now
Is someone smacking a carpet
Far off, beyond the water tanks,
And very faintly
Children's cries.

There's no more need
To run aslant the world.

*

Meanwhile, elsewhere : 'I don't care
A kick of a hen,' says this one.
'The cold clank of the bucket handle,
The rat running on the wall,
My mother who hasn't a step in her since
She broke her thigh, the turf-smoke
And my face concealed in it —
All these are good enough.'

Another : 'Let us stop heroic
Lies and allegory. Too many
Statues have baton and blank eyes
Directed over the market-place;
Even the emblems — eagle, winged lion —
Of Evangelists, fail
To convince me : I prefer
A plover in a field,
The cat curled in a grocer's shop.'

The waves of Galilee have furled
Rose-imaged oleanders
For an age. Along the shore
Magdala, a mud village with fowls,
Has forgotten Mary. Women
Now help deepen rough red furrows,
Making a heritage,

An orchard crop, for boys and girls
Pale-haired under this sun
Instead of dark as ghettoes.

Each day is dependable and
Controlled, like an office clock; steady
As some figure with black skirt
And black umbrella you see move
Among the cloches, orderly,
In rain of Paris suburbs.
Reason, in charge of itself, craves
To build new colonnades of thought,
Or prove a spangle-lit
Fresh spark of theory, or free
Old proverbs from the humped *tels*.

*

If one could see beyond house fronts
Into the past, as through a pane
Of glass, the tremendous roar, then quiet,
Of dying in rubble would be plain.
But beams and bricks are up again.

Under Crimean harbour depths,
What silent traffics go between
Sunk Greek galleys, green swaying weed
On marbles of the Chersonese,
Out-of-date warships, rebel cruiser,
Engine parts of every kind
And bones odd sizes — all of these
Washed like cockles of the sea?

In streets where paper blows about,
A stab goes through me of the talk
That brought disastrous happenings,
The death of feeling that I caused.
Urchins playing give a shout
And the thought leaves me as I walk.

*

Gone is anything sick, sad or fanciful.
What moved me was the hand of the Mechanized Chessman,
Horror and mystery in his stuffy robes.
What I've been through was the Hall of Mirrors,
Distorting mirrors of a fair. What I've seen
Were obscene freaks in a sawdust pit,
And scenes painted with size, swollen
The size of hallucinations —
All believed in at the time,
All suffered as one suffers
The anaesthetic dream
Of spiritual blessedness,
Of spirals choiring :
Then afterwards,
The fit of weeping.

*

There's a small hill on the Bog of Allen
With jackdaws and beeches and a square house.
The maids are by the fire. They sew and speak
Of a cousin, or how to help the niece,
Or will Dolan sell, or of the boy
One of them went with (as she bites a thread),
Or else the time long back when they found
An empty can of tea and some sandwiches
Wrapped up in a *Freeman's Journal*, and left
By the ambush there must have been at the gates
(And the mistress in bed seeing on the wall
The flash of the fired barracks across the way);
And will her great-grandchildren, they wonder,
Take after their da?
                        It's to be hoped they will,
Thinks their mother (keeper of all things
Who has watched her children sleep) who now watches them
With her husband making a garden bonfire.
He's grinning and swearing under his breath
And tearing his coat and telling them how to help.
Screaming, happy in doing something

And bringing the wrong sticks, they'll now and again
Take fright at the blaze, run away to her, then
Forget and dash back to add more. She looks
At their napes, at the back of their knees, and sighs :
How to guard them from danger, from fear,
For ever? The dogs go off to sniff and to hunt
On their own. Smoke tingles and eddies
Through sparks of laughter, gusts of seriousness
That are insubstantial and flickering
To anyone else — but to her, solid
And round as the brick oasthouse in the yard.

*

Leaf upon earth, and loam under the frame,
And pear, espaliered, nailed across a wall;
The chatter of small-territoried birds,
Or a staked plant that where it blooms will fall;
The fly crawling up a stem it hugs;
Beetles that drag their carapace, alone,
Intent, through thickest grass where groundbees drone;
A swan that dents her breast against an edge
Of lake, her feet now softly on the ooze
And now her bill nudging in roots of sedge —
These are my kin (she well might cry), their labours
Are my days and reasoning : as strong
And logical as Schoolmen after long
Disorder, wreckage and dark anarchy.

*

We will now do the linen. The weight of it, lifted out of
        deep drawers
    And cool to the touch, and the warm smell when it's taken
    Out of the airing cupboard, give me a pride
That any woman has felt who's putting a room to rights,
    Scrubbing as if herself were being scrubbed,
    Scouring as if her soul were being scoured,
Straightening up and sorting as if in her own mind.
    (My helper, bending her neck, shows tendrils of hair

[67]

That surely her friend, who has his bicycle propped
This instant against the ivied wall, admires. Let him wait.)

How good
To spice and flavour well; to walk the dim and white
    And dairy-smelling passages; to look
On harbours, as in Boston, when the fishermen are home
    (Their boats are *Evie II* and *Maria Soccorsa*
    With dories slung on the pilot-house roof, the snow
Filling them) — to be safe, and have enough for the fire.
    Or beside other quays where in markets, we women,
    Scarf-faced and red-fingered, must sell fish :
This is also good, the mist mingling with our breath
    In gossip and curses, to rid us of old shames
    And old mistakes that make us groan at night.

*

Crones stop in the street and mumble
    In each others' faces;
    Their grandsons are masons perched
    And painting overhead;
    Their nieces are washerwomen
    By stones of some broad rivermouth
    Dried to a middle trickle.
In a room with drawn blinds
    Loneliness is consoled
    Between covers of the Bible :
    Often you only have to grasp
    The book to feel worthy.
D'you notice how old women
    Who have missed a destroying
    Happiness look away?
    Whereas the old and plain who meet
    Your eyes, do so because
    They know they are more holy,
    Or else more powerful —
Even if they've acquired

[68]

A look of snapped twigs, or hollow
Beetle-sherds, or gnawed
Husks, or have about them
A faint, discernible smell
Of mouldering earth and deadness.

But growing girls : slow airs
Of cowslip warmth blow from you.
  Some, whose pairs
Of breasts are tightly met
Together as young apples,
  Will perhaps get
Caught by gasp and relish
Of mock struggle, and
  Become a prudish
Housewife or a drudge or
Slattern. You, the rest —
  Whatever your
Demeanour, epoch, dress
And voice, timid or dowried
  Ones no less
Than waif or heroine —
Are sisterly to those
  Who moved in muslin
On a tender lawn;
Who left the art-room, its chill
  Casts undrawn;
Outgrew a corridor
Of pianos practising
  In muffled war;
And who forgot the yew
As hiding-place. Your state
  Is strange, new,
Unhurried as the run
Of angels, neither ended
  Nor begun;
Your thought the shape and shade
Of soft air through a marble
  Balustrade :

Untried and unexpressed,
You wish for marvels, danger,
  Deeds unguessed.

*

If I could be like Niobe,
Mother of many, before the vengeance,
My robes brimming out with goodness,
Filled with content. . . . But I cannot.
Something weak and nagging in me
Causes me to turn my head,
After a time, at any noise
Coming from far off, carried
By the wind from places where,
If you're in trouble, the old whore
And the old soldier, blunt, blowsy,
Plain as plain, are to be utterly
Trusted; where philosophies
Are arguments it's best to forget
Or else to remake each hour, and feel
Alter with a change of light,
With new work started, or the sound
Of sudden wet, below, in the street.
Lately, I notice that the flattened
Saints no longer burn their windows
But are idle and remote;
And I can't bear to watch the winter
Smokiness on playing-fields;
Or poverty, like a goat in its range
Over the common, along the waste :
And though ill-humour and a certain
Haste now hover in the air,
The day dangles an empty bridle.

*

'Hidden in the womb I lie
With beating heart and closed eye,
Thinking forward, casting back,
Through our living almanac.
Covered in as warm a tide
As this, and lapped from side to side,
I was washed in altered forms
By huge calms and vaster storms
Of that primal, misty sea
Tasting of futurity.
Gone my gills — but see their cleft —
Long before the Alps were left
Higher than the lakes which fell
Into gloom of bitter spell.
I have been near scale and quill,
Furry chine is with me still;
Seen the rocks and plains dissolved,
Seasons, heavens, aims revolved;
I have reaped bread from a weed;
Searched to find out every need
Of my horror or my trust,
Ecstasies, constraint, disgust
And rebellion. Fortified
By great portents, I have tried —
Using all my brain and force,
All my will, all my resource —
To shape my life within a scene
Already known. In truth, I've been
Vain as cities, poor as hills,
Travelled through such endless ills,
Through such hope and fear and rage
For an unremembered age,
That I beat my prisoned fist,
Angered that when I untwist
From this closeness into air
Final and fulfilling, there
I must barter, prate and mime
For a pulse, a blink of time.'

*

How we hate each other
In a narrow room,
　We terrible knitters
　Under the lamp;
How we knot and lace
The hours interminable,
　Intricate and
　Pale as in
The Book of Kells, we nuns
And all unmothers of men;
　Or we who look
　At backs of houses
As we sit and stitch,
Crowded elbow to side,
　Handling the stuff
　And stiff brocade
Of death : for that is how
It seems to us who stifle
　Here, bound
　By a weight of days;
How we regret not seeing
Leaves in an approaching
　Storm fly up;
　And how we envy
Those who rustle
In their silks, and thread
　Few words with looks
　Brilliantly false, before
They praise, and thank,
And yawn to bed.

*

Solomon kept chariot horses
Stabled under Temple walls.
They stamped within their hollow stalls.

I must escape, I must avoid
The puckered mouth and twitching thumb
Of Age who waits for me to come.

[72]

Swifts flicker round the sill,
Beat their shadows on the blind,
Beat their hurry in the mind.

*

She has reached
The rim of time
The dune end
Of the world.
Spiked grass
Loose sand
What to lean on
Where to turn . . .
Something recalled
Before it is known,
Old as the ground
New as herself
But sharp and steep
As memories
Of crag and shelf
In witless sheep
Who make a mountain
Track on lowly
Downs, of rushing
Winds in birds
Who now are placid
On the green
But once were wilder
Than the air —
Some voice in her
That tries to find
And utter the old
Chants, the old
Pain, cries out :

*

O random Fate, who rout
And shatter and unbind
The elbow-leaning, tame,
Demurest pieties —
Free me that I may wear
A yoke I hanker for
And name : precise belief
In the authority
And overbearing deeds
Of a loved mortal, one
Whose strength and tongue shall be
The provenance of right;
A part in all transactions
Of his mind and any
Tragedies which follow.
Admit that the devout
Must have sanction from Church,
A thief from others' failings,
The privileged from custom,
Scholar from book — and I
From discipline of great
And terrible truths. Hold me,
Pour back my soul, let me know
Life the unfinished : so
Reflood the desolate ebb :
Renew me, make me whole.

A Cloud Across the Sun

1949

IRELAND

This is the country
That has no desolation, no empty feel
(The pagan kings are always there)
In ruined abbey, ruined farmhouse,
Slab of cromlech, or a wheel
Travelling a bog road
Through Calary's too quiet air.

NO ENTRY

1

When Hector's foot comes creaking on a stair,
Or Helen's breath steams in the frozen air,
  Moments that no one ever sang :
  These are the hidden places where
    I move about and find
    Some freshness for the mind,
  A gap to be explored with care,
As over David's harp in a dark corner
Runs a mouse and gives it a small twang.

2

Constricted space ! Others, I know, have wide
Imaginary fields where they confide
  Their dreams and where they roam at ease —
  For little Hamnet hasn't died,
    But makes a swing with other
    Children; look, Leander
  Steps out backward from the tide —
Not only dreams but systems of escape
As furious or everyday as these :

[75]

3

She's thin and sallow. The headmistress pays
Her meanly to curb the English pupils' ways:
   Tenez-vous convenablement.
  Outside, a château park decays
    With drifting leaves, in spite
    Of drifting girls. . . . Then flight
To her room — the *Nuit de Mai* — to gaze
At the full-bosomed Muse, the poet's brow
And welling sadness — *Ah, quel ravissement!*

4

Young Ted, the garden boy, unsmilingly
Will trench and stake and dig. I'll lay a ready
  Bet he'd never swear or fight —
  With summer hanging heavily,
    Or autumn smelling sour,
    When colder winds scour
  The earth, or shoots break out. Instead he
Glows, he burns from direst sin's repentance
While he shouts and moans on Chapel night.

5

That tramp, dirty as the London soil,
Hugs a park bench, his hideous face a foil
  To children, birds and dogs, whose scufflings
  He's too motionless to spoil.
    Let the weak winter sun
    Show the tree's skeleton,
  The sharp leaves' scurry and recoil,
And daze his red-rimmed eyes and part his lips
As peace swoops to him on her pigeon wings.

6

Or other ways of sidling, groping back
From the affront of living. Almanac,
  Great pyramid and portent turn
  The sluggard-rolling zodiac

Into 'What month, dear, were
You born?' and 'Now it's clear :
   We add. . . .' The invisible tide is slack
And lost Atlantis silent; but those ears
Catch auguries which drown them in concern.

                    7

Even the Libyan Arabs take retreat
To their Green Mountain, up a thousand feet,
   Their grazing lands. But I'm shut out :
   No entry, even by deceit;
      Not with my eyes clamped tight
      Against the speckled night;
   And never in my work, whose beat
Hurts with its knock and actual daily pulse
Of stinging joy, short ease and constant doubt.

                ANY TROUBLED AGE

O mussel coloured houses by the dunes
With fluttered boats feeling among the shoals,

      How many times can it have happened,
      How many times

O mountain straked and softened by blue air
With trickles fingering between the reeds,

      How many times can it have happened,
      How many times

O cottage field warmed by the breath of sheep
When rain begins to gossip in the hedge,

      How many times will woman see
      Some man trudging

To the door, and rise, with a broken welcome —
For the whole news has travelled in his eyes.

                   [77]

A pillar wrecked
By sand; the slat
Of softest leaves
To hide a voice
And hint its echo;
Pediments
Where hogmaned ponies
Prance in fat
Of stubbornness;
Or the stones
Of Clonmacnois,
Lichen-flecked;
Cupolas that
Burst through snow;
Spires where angels
Catch their gowns;
Tin-roofed chapels
In sick towns —
A choice,
A guess.

ANALOGUE

Men who care for the slow
Headswinging walk of a bull;
Whose hopes and dread rise
In the blade, bend with a stalk;
Who will explain each whim
Of angered, joking Fate
By marrying season to proverb;
Their hands knotted and learned
In lifting a pick; who know
How pain and weather can baulk
All plans : such folk, when dear
Demeter's ground lay warm

[78]

And dry with almond husks
And myrtle and would owe
Remembrance to the dead,
Argued, as men today
Talk, in *The Barley Mow,*
Of ghosts and penalties.

Men whose faces are stern,
For the rungs shake under them
As they climb different ladders
To consolation, and turn
In dispute or vertigo :
'Credo,' they call like birds,
Then, 'Curro.' Aware of doctrine
And the great hazard of words,
Their skin creeping, their nerves
Taut in effort to learn
For certain the logic of grace :
Beside a gas-fire, in cloister,
Study or abbey — shut off
By intellect from the day,
Not heeding if last night's rain
Harmed or was southerly kind
To the breeding earth — their concern
Is souls and punishment.

ROSS ABBEY

The cowpat track and dusty bramble leads
To childhood's riverwet and glistening meads.
O dear Ross Abbey ! ruined, with a tree
Grown through you, how your presence lived in me
With images, persistent and devout,
Of brother, weed and water, frog and trout,
Until that middle-aged, that rainy day
I saw you once again, then looked away.

[79]

John the Baptist stood with hair
Blown through by the morning air.
Calloused, lean as thorns and brown,
Over the bare land and down
The listening ear of time he spoke
A prologue nothing can revoke.

John, the son of Zebedee,
From the sweet Tiberian sea
With its kingfishers and quail
And oleanders, rips the veil
Of laziness. Through streets the crowd
Argues with him strong and loud.

John, asleep at Ephesus,
Stir your jaws and pray for us !
Pilgrims to your holy ground,
We're dazed by love, already bound,
And waiting to be subtly kissed :
O preacher and Evangelist.

John of Patmos, round your isle
Waves clash and suns revile
As you mouth, with roughened lips,
A barbarous Apocalypse —
Great visions of a lunatic
Who finds a world convulsed and sick.

First, vague prophetic sounds;
Till a fisherman astounds;
Then a contemplative love
Transcending what all deeds may prove.
If last, disintegration's fire
Should come, we've seen four men's desire.

ORIGINS

I

Into the past, I guess my way
To find out from what line I'm bred :
To black tents of a restless brood,
A curdled sky, unending plains,
Horses stamping in a cold
Hard as were the Nails folks say
The gipsies forged. Or still more old
And doubtful : to a vanished mark
Of some forgotten town whose men,
In rustle of silvered silks, unshadowed
Night during a faint dog's bark.

2

Then later — pedlar, diplomat,
Landlord, peasant — these speak low,
Whistle, curse, stamp their feet;
That one greasy as his hat,
This one laughing from conceit.
Mine. As for the women : some
Have a scent of melancholy sedge,
Or laurels in wet woods; others
Rock slowly on high balconies
Under a charring sun; and some
Are rags along a gutter's edge.

3

Could quick, varied contradiction
Of a mood or thought, derive
From fancies they were racked with — could
It stem from their belief in arches
Made of angels' wings, from fret
Of learning, or from schemes sad
As rain that falls from winter larches?
And some ghastly call of wit
Come from where there was a joke
Before a murder — now where flit
Jackdaws in the ivied tower?

4

Beyond huge silting up and tracts
In time, appear the paradisal
Leaves : this moist and sheltering sight
Of the great garden, dense, entire
With fruit all year, and flying lizards
Settling in the tree of life,
Wings folded; and the sweet thorn-apple
Sharpening minds into a knife —
This land which none need go from, past
The distant, guardian sword of fire
That wavers to the left and right.

5

But if an earlier age lay northward
Of the dank Caucasian pass,
Before the everburning fields
And Tartarus the triple-moated
Town, and near the iron-throated
Mountain coughing brass and steel —
Then, as a woman, I have found
What we inherit in our blood
From those bereaved by the first wastes
And wailing for their menfolk drowned
In utter darkness of that flood.

WHILE SATYRS HUNTED FOR A NYMPH

While satyrs hunted for a nymph
As we for strawberries in a wood,
Philosophers, their blood and lymph
Excited by the search for Good,

Found Cause in Space; and tracked Despair
In Time; felt human Destiny
And Reason swaying in the air
Like a bee-tumbled peony;

Perceived (but never told their School)
Truth transparent as a shrimp
Darting backwards in a pool;
And Thought with all its tendons limp.

They are gone. Their counter-pleas
Of proof have left us, every one,
Like sailors whistling for a breeze —
And still the breeze drops with the sun.

EVEN SO

In spite of striding
Lean-legged John's
Flame of words
In the wilderness;

And orators
Who stand in bronze,
Braving both
The rain and birds —

None the less,
Just as dogs
Must always lap
At filthy puddles,

So the fishwives'
Hands will chap,
Roofs fall loose
And walls get sick.

In spite of garlic
Breath of Rome
And senators;
In spite of lives

Good as fables;
Envoys, tired
And fidgeting
At treaty tables —

Children still
Have pecked-out lungs;
The old maid slanders
All around;

Hope like a fox,
Has gone to ground;
And crowds feel hate
That burns their tongues.

POISONED IN SEARCH OF THE MEDICINE OF IMMORTALITY

When Hsüang Tsung, great emperor,
Giddy and ill, carried in a litter,
Saw the stars sway,

His conquests and his arguments
And powers, falling into fever with him,
Pulsed their lives away.

Bow to his shade. To be at rest
Is but a dog that sighs and settles : better
The unrelenting day.

EPIPHANY IN A COUNTRY CHURCH

Rough-fisted winter and the blurred organ join
In minds of villagers to bring
A smell of wheatstraw under hoofs and sanfoin
In hay where beasts are fattening.

What does it matter if our wise men stress
The Barn as false, the Feast as wrong?
I hold the Magi were the wiser, yes,
To be believed in for so long.

A January mist now hides the wood;
Hard facts are overlaid by myth :
In us these last keep company, and should,
Like heart and bones in Farmer Smith,

Who kneels to pray. Rubbing his neck — If beef
Goes up this month, he thinks. . . . Round him
Confer vague consolations, powers of grief,
Man's fear and the high cherubim.

WAR AND PEACE

'Lately I cried with men.
Now once again
I wait for the slack of the tide,
Watch for a smooth in the wave and drop
My lobsterpots
Down between the grey rocks :
In the wet rope
Strong hope.

'The violence I was in,
Its crash and din
Are gone. My dear one, nothing breaks
When she holds it or tumbles from her lap
Save when she starts up
Quickly to greet me or give me to sup :
In the folds of her dress
Gentleness.'

[85]

ON LOOKING DOWN A STREET

My mind's disturbed as rooks in the air. . . .
May a thin-shouldered mountain hare
Or shy and meditative donkey,
Cat that gallops down an alley
And the squint-eyed, sandy dab,
Curlew, spider, vole and crab —
Creatures both severe and great
Or nimble as hens running under a gate —
Pray for me now. Lord, how I need
Their cleverness, their careful speed
Or power to be still, their sense,
Their pride and total innocence !
To keep from being fool or wretch
Till the hearse-horses trot this stretch.

ALTER EGO

Mephisto and the Wandering Jew,
Ghost and gombie, witch and hoodoo :
    These are a tin cat-head
    Trembling on a thread
To frighten birds! The devil's brew
That does exist, stirs in you.

No malediction neared your crib;
Yet underneath the vaulted rib
    And flip-flap of your lungs,
    Darkly as in dung's
Warmth, there breeds and grows the glib
Cruelty that moves a nib,

Beats a dog, aims a gun,
Maims the Father, kills the Son,
    Infects a realm, and haunts
    The body with such taunts
And horrors that you shriek Be done . . .
I know, for you and I are one.

A Kite's Dinner

1954

EVERYMAN IN THE WILDERNESS

'Our own God travelled in his Ark
In step with us, by day, by dark.
The little landcrabs scuttled by
Like fears, transparent and too sly
For us to glimpse their homes. Our feet
Moved in scant grass; then manna, sweet
And trembling on the branch, was left
For boulders, shale and scree and cleft
Which, gasping, we yet had to climb . . .'
Such was their song. O cheating Time !
You will not, while the world unrolls
A curious design for souls,
Help those who have been glancing back
On old Egyptian wrongs and the black
Bruise of guilt for even longer
Than the Jews : you still defer
That green peace and the crops and sheep
Men see ahead and crave to keep.

A TUSCAN FARMER

Why praise the huge past works of Hercules
When he leans idly on his club in Rome?
Come to my farm instead; walk round my home
When autumn puts its ladder in the trees
And what was stripped two thousand years ago
Is stripped again, or ploughed, made into stacks
And ricks and bundled heaps, by arms and backs
Aching with thrift. The least of plants that grow
As fodder have to fight the drought : my oxen,
Going softly, pull with as great a strain.

Each clod, and hanging leaf, and wild grass cane
Is stronger than that strongest of all men
Whose lion, hydra, hell-dog, mares and boar
Were overcome indeed, but once, no more.

LINES FOR THE MARGIN OF AN OLD GOSPEL

Children now awake to birds.
  Mortals rose to words
    Fresh as the morning

When clover and the far hawks,
  Scabious and meadow-larks
    Shadowed a searing

That ran along nerve and sense,
  To mend a bad conscience
    By caustic of loving.

Tax-collector and prostitute :
  Perhaps they were astute,
    More understanding

Than open throats, festered teeth,
  Slovenly wits and breath
    Gaping and crowding,

Or than any tolling-tongued
  Masters who had wronged
    Life with their learning.

Gently or fiercely, to all around
  He would explain, expound,
    Like a dog leaping

Through tall stalks of wheat :
  Such was the pounce and feat
    Of this debating;

[88]

Till an attic room rang
  With a sad air sung
    After the supping.

Destiny and darkness flow
  Faster, now, than low
    Clouds that are falling;

His friends must snore, head to rock;
  The world takes stock,
    Hardly breathing.

Thinking how steepled jealousy,
  Prim-lipped authority,
    Pride of condemning

Can derive from that despair,
  Sleep, lantern, unfair
    Act of denying,

Warmth drains out of us. The soul
  Shown in its goodness, whole :
    No hammering

Of flesh to wood can harm that proof.
  Yet man is without roof
    And night is freezing.

A CLERICAL SQUIRE

    Warm by the fire,
    Toe in slipper,
    Swinging his foot :
    A clerical squire.
    Where did he pass?
    Outside, the Dipper
    Ignores the spire.
    Cold as brass,
    Sour as soot,
    Are death and desire.

CALENDAR

1

Too clean, the infant year, too new
And snowy innocent; it hides from view
Old rooted grudge and sin.

2

But memory floods to an edge
Of dark and bitter February sedge
That shivers like our skin,

3

And doubts are colder than the hands
Of men who harrow the long pasturelands
In painful discipline :

4

Until high mercy will assuage
The heart, and show it April's missal-page
Alive upon the ground.

5

Lovers now welcome thunderskies :
Their shock, the shelter, and a flash of eyes
That can be strange, profound,

6

Then tender as the fledgling days
Of June, when beauty trembles in the haze
With every rustling sound.

7

The halfway month. A pause for fears
Of middle-age, a deskful of arrears,
Time sped, so little done,

8

As heat lies heavy on the land.
Dogs snap at flies. Few tempers can withstand
The slowness of the sun,

9

Those parks that shrivel, leaves that spoil,
The sad allotments dug in a sour soil
Where towns and grime have won :

10

We need to feel gross sacks of grain
And in them, deities of earth and rain,
To put our sickness right.

11

The cake has crumbled, fires are lit.
Pink-pawed and back humped up, a mouse will sit
And nibble in quick fright,

12

And old, fat-fingered oaks are bare
While stars wheel through the empty, frozen air
To the slow hum of night.

THE HUNTER

Now show me any whole truth
Sustained as summer was in youth,
Plain and bare as winter trees,
Glittering like Ligurian seas,
Found in haycocks and in spires
Or lapping under hawser wires,
Burnt by meteor, scratched by fowl,
Alive in nudge and grin and scowl,
Proud as rags that sit alone,

Stronger than a dolmen stone,
As impertinent and wild
As a rough-haired tinker's child,
Sudden, like a gannet's dive,
Yet close and warm as honey-hive.

Because an old, obsidian face
Looks down in disillusioned grace;
Because, with pebbles spurting fear,
Siddhartha and his charioteer,
Fleeing through moonlight, found decay
And death and suffering on their way;
Because a half-wheel pulls a bell
And half a truth will serve to tell
Bewildered people; and a flash
Of dazzling knowledge gave one gash
To time when the great Doctor saw
His tomes, his tomes summed up as straw :
Shall I not ransack, search and tear
The clouds and grasses with my snare?

The Leaves Darken
1964

DARKNESS

And what will mitigate my life's long fault,
  I beg you, if authority's black stuffs
  Should fail to reconcile me
  To the final blindfold?
  Cassock and blackboard
  Are under the same burden,
  Suffer the same problem, as ourselves;
  While conscience comes at night and stings
  The darkness : much as Carthage, ploughed under,
  Was then sown with salt.
A conjuror's cloak; the Queen of Spades
  With her poor migraine face : these
  Are for innocence : it waits agog,
  For flourishes of fireworks to exalt
  A pitchblack sky. Later,
  Incredible beliefs, the greatest things
  Given to the soul, are only
  Metaphors or hints
  Taken from lovers when they meet
  Bemused, in gardens,
  Among mooncast shadows
  Denser than a vault.
Let me predict my funeral weather
  Biting at black coats,
  With the new box — cave dark and cupboard thick —
  Brought to a lurching halt
  Near brambles and tipped headstones in the family
  Burial ground, and flurryings
  Of shocked and interrupted jackdaws. . . .

With so much still unlearned, ignored;
So many moments of compassion skimped
By me or lost; this private graveyard seems
An apt memorial, with its church a ruin,
And its quiet cracked
By the quick clatter of black wings
In crude assault.

ON BEING OF ONE'S TIME

I

Thistle lances are now broken
Through the winter woods, in a past tense
Of quarrels greenly spoken.
And the clock jerks on; each cog engaged,
Each weight, each wheel tied by obedience
And well caged.
That plain-faced clock whose stare
Is a big cheat,
Reminding me how eyes
Of men selling a horse will meet
One's glance in a fine honest glare
For the gigantic lies.

2

Keep step with tick and chime? But histories
In their divergence and entanglement
Force their own pulse to beat
Along my arteries,
Hobbling, racing ahead, or in retreat
From that odd ghost, the present.
Mountain among mountains, showing
Grey as its low raincloud overhead,
Mycenae lours
As if the murderous story were unsaid
And the warm air, at Aulis, waiting
In windless patience, knew the hours.

Am I committed purely to the moment?
No, with carved Hittite kings flaying
Prisoners alive (a thought abhorrent
As a fallout dread);
Fish-eaten Shelley rolling with the tide;
The twelvepenny dagger still in Marlowe's forehead;
And my nose twitching
From the flesh Spain burnt. Small wonder Zeno
And his arrow rused
Whole ages; while Plotinus, in a great stride
Of reason, fretted about Time : its flow,
And if what's at our throats, and gone, are fused.

CARTOGRAPHY

I

To map out man or woman,
Let your nervous hand try to lead
Wisdom by a twisted forelock.
Find what injuries were done
To self-esteem : redress
The boundary; give fads attention.
Measure out loneliness.
If you hold the plan
Still workable, think how a weathercock
Will rule an empty street at night;
Or that a smudge of print can cite
Full extravagancies
Waiting in a grub; or plant-seed;
Or the mind —
Wild as equinoctial seas —
Of ordinary humankind.

A boat slewed
Towards the urgent flood,
Its anchor fluke dragging mud
And cable fouled : that goes for most of us. We risk
Mishandling time, whose hurry
Carries off branch, bole, root, in spate.
I've watched rank pulled away, near tamarisk
And the Bermudian tides, where a proconsul made
Gestures too old and negligent;
And there, known a massive brain prematurely
Crumble in wrecker's dust;
Learnt how young sailors dropped, beside a carronade
And hulk, on sand : no moment
Being right or just.
While coral of praise or gratitude
(You've guessed) can come too late.

Does this smack
Overmuch of water? But one's
Life can be a voyage
To Cythera : in black
Storms; faint calm; or else uneasy from cross-currents
Of what's difficult and fluent.
As there's no finish to our quirks, beliefs,
Distorted theories and failing reasons,
We might embark
For coasts that wear a greener plume,
Where caverns rest the mind in dark,
Leaving a crystal-shattered spume
Outside. No light can gauge
Hollows and sudden gaps, or chart
Those devious reefs
And unsure soundings in a person's heart.

CONTINUITY

When morning came lightly as a hare's breath,
Worry held us
In its copper snare
With a sick pull of death.
We were alone
Under the anger of old people and their
Bias. Now, walking crookedly,
We're mottle-red;
Shrunk or paunchy;
Brittle as curled-up leaves; or rancorous;
Others ghastly,
Like a bone :
Fearing our sons and their bold, brilliant stare.

YOUTH AND AGE

I

Comfort is small as a snipe's heart to a child,
The world suspect,
And laughter a snickering of knives.
This boy, with hair curled tight as any faint, distant
Forest of hung tapestry,
Has thoughts that quickly dip and rise like finches in flight.
No pedant, no burnt pod
Of learning, can deflect him while he moves
Apart, in a thin
Simple air, hardy as a saint,
With the same triumph.

2

Mountain mists both frenzy and suffuse him,
Till they melt
Into vast torpor, a bored dream.
He might—as Bruce's heart in a box was thrown into battle—
Offer his adored a rose,

[97]

Alone, in a closed garden and with trembling knees.
Such youthful Lists of Love,
Which become jest and rage and bullying,
Can make him use
The extreme and hermit right to pray and fast,
Ignored, on rocks.

3

Oaths of yesterday are stale, sickly
As hawthorn smell.
Big in his strength, he'll stride bare hills,
Then ripening lowlands, to where dykes, ports and tides
Control the State, commerce, one's life.
Honesty may turn or quit; argument's useless.
He must learn to rig
His balance-pans of pride and skills, and make
The debit less,
The honour large : liking to take or give
With mastery.

4

So cool the summer and so dull the fair,
He sits, afraid,
Under his armorial tree
While its dry branches creak and rattle like a relic
Of his anger as he shakes
A stick. Veins knot, and arteries are choked, to know
The years so burdensome
Or else too light, too null. Those sly and laughing
Children who played
Near have run : they're gone from his weak sight
And feebler tears.

FOR MY DEAD FRIENDS

1

Fit for a knacker's yard,
This carcase of a poor
Parthenon, purged and marred,
Is such a prodigy,
None can feel condescending. From its floor,
Where wagtails run and dip
In marble puddles after morning rain,
Columns empower the air with flesh,
Not stone, tender and fresh :
Making a pain
Of exultation grip
The midriff-soul with love.
Where to turn, giddy from shock?
Below, a woman spins, shouts to a neighbour;
Children play. High, high above,
Sea-eagles, circling slowly, eye with disfavour
Any shell left chipped and empty
On a rock.

2

Taking stock, we can
Jot down that in no matter what ironic
Landscape people work and die —
The serious, foolish, modest, lewd,
The bold or shy, violent or subdued,
With their diversity of features,
Humours, failures —
They have renewed
Their pity and are found
Forgiving God each tragic,
Tearing thing,
Throat swollen and voice faltering
From gratitude.
What more should I,
Muddled and earthbound,
Need for the soul's nourishment?

3

In spite of which I waste
My breath, and spill live sorrow on the thought
That we, who carry friends
Like a good taste
In the mouth, so short a time, ought
To be left, not random odds and ends
For a remembrance, not a shard
Stupidly small and hard,
But an emphatic plier
That can wrench the mind, turn it and amaze;
Some elegiac force
Whose lunge and potency
Could lather Phaethon's reins, each horse
Sun-bent though undisastrously :
More than Achilles felt when mountain flanks
Showed muletracks, scarred all sideways,
To get planks
To feed Patroclus' fire.

4

The pen scratches and flies drone
And towns suffer heat,
And I know life can be weariness
And the sour pleasure of the incomplete.
To ease it calls for metaphor.
I'll take, then, for my own
Hand, the Parthenon, that hollowness
Above new Athens, quite distinct
From the complexity
Spread out beneath, but linked
With every roof and hearth, as what is true
Should be; that shell
Now flushed by haze, colour of asphodel —
And pick it up, and hold it to my ear
Whenever, privately, I wish to hear
Its murmur celebrate
Those whom I knew
Who were both good and great.

A QUERY

Rusted, small, weed-hidden
And unlocked, forgotten :
Such was the backdoor
Of the unbelievable Byzantine citadel.
So when Turks elbowed through it, grunting, to dispel
This blaze unseen before —
A jewel-hung emperor as Christ Pantocrator —
Who were the faithful, who the infidel?
Experts are cunning and say nothing more.

WHEN MOORE FIELD WAS ALL GRAZED

When Moore field was all grazed
And Finnesburie ploughed,
People were fiery, clever, glum or crazed;
Hard knuckled; and proud
Liars; and well-phrased.

REVELATION

Tinker

Proud as a Paleologue, whose ninety
Thousand frying pans
His forbears had to patch,
This rogue stares

Full at my eyes, aloof, in scorn.
Rags and raindrops catch
In the hedge, to show his kind
Despise and hate

Roof or chair or chimney cowl,
But need to share some narrow
Edge with slug and beetle,
Thorn and frog.

His blunt-nosed women, heavy shawled
And still as stones, gaze
At their whippet bitch that trembles,
Lame. Why then

Have fear and shame crawled up my bones,
Until he turns to crack
Twigs and get the sopping
Ditch ablaze?

Tailor

Crouchback, with a crunch of scissors,
On a bare, hard floor,
He fills his mind with shadows.
Some are kind

As the old whispering leaves of Mamre;
Some could fold behind
A door in ghettos; others
Are charred years

Of being outcast; tears; and a vast
Final heap that wastes
And heaves at Dachau, nearly
Dead. ' "Judge not. . . .

' "Be a lover of peace, a maker of peace. . . ." '
He bastes a thread. Back bent,
It must not tire. 'And Hillel
Also said :

' "In my abasement is exaltation." '
The tailor lifts his eyes.
All pain is black : they glow,
They run with fire.

Soldier

Time's a thief; and terror comes
By mouthfuls, with a roar
Of drums; until a bleat
Of musketry

Makes Grief go hooded down the street
And Hunger tug her shawl.
The soldier : did he shiver
When he gained,

Then spilled, the tumbling walls of fortress
Tiryns — (only magpies,
Now, and milk-veined thistles
Warm its heart) —

Or wrenched Jerusalem apart?
He'll cackle in the pub, tell
Lies, and rub a stiffness
Of the knees.

His children play at marbles, or they
Sing : 'We won't surrender,
We won't surrender, you king
Of the Barbarees.'

Sailor

In a dream of dolphin calm,
He can feel monsters gleam
And maul, deep under bow
And keel; and crabs

Slide to the turn and fall of tide,
Where caves weep, and rocks
Burn, and oceans glint
Like silverfoil.

Now for the dogwatch mandolin,
With tunes of sunset, home
And tears : the sailor's debt
To all his dears,

Before a strong shuddering lurch and foam
Through which his vessel raves
And slats; till hawsers pull
At quays that hint

Complexity, flaw, unease,
In black winds along wharfs
Where stocks of goods spoil
And rats gnaw.

Rich man

He jokes and humphs with dignities
Of robes, smoothness of jaws,
Huge shade of palaces
And strength of laws;

While tongues of lie and gossip guess
His powers, where they reach
And how they're swayed. Now
He provokes despair,

Now showers gold. His gardeners, high
On rungs, who pleach and clip,
Hold his commands to mean
There should be nothing

To reproach in green, or to
Confute in gilt. Fountains,
Gates, are filled by crowds,
Shuffling and mute;

While rivergods, who had to turn
To figured stone, forget
The weed and spotted loach,
And tilt their urn.

Poor man

Mistrust, by a small cough, betrays
Its loneliness, as through
The dusk, a frightened tap
Of heels hurries

Past crimes a gate or privet hedge
Or curtain-net conceals,
Days are a slap in the mouth,
A kick in the crutch,

From citizens so virtuous,
Suburban and polite,
They'd hate to touch this creature
Who'll pick up

Fag ends from gutters, with no mind
To work or please or care.
Let their souls rot (he mutters
As he bends)

For being unaware of seas
That lie behind the brimming
Tears and red-net eyeballs
Of a sot.

Beggarman

Grincing on a yellow fiddle
In a town where gulls
And grime mix in the air's
Familiar chime

For priest and bookie, Dooley's Bar,
Swans and sticks and dead old
Buckets on the Liffey
Mud, — he knows

Men turn their head away when walking
Past, and flush in the cold,
As if their breath or blood
Had a catarrh

So vehement, it made them choke
To brush against the Four Last
Things of death, judgement,
Heaven and hell.

For who of us can tell what pride
Or freedom may yet croak
For pennies on the windy,
Wet kerbside?

Thief

No footfall. Not a squeak of a hinge.
But midnight has been stabbed;
The core of the house prised
And grabbed. Weak

And sore, you feel that hands have fumbled
Your heart's cage. At a price
He's caught. You rage. But still
He understands :

'Perhaps you forget. My counterpart
Was set up to fulfil
A prophecy, was promised
Paradise.'

THE LEAVES DARKEN

If a child's tale were sung
To kings and the tired spearmen;
Or if Outer Isles, fog-blind,
Are found only by raven
Croaks; or a new housing scheme must geld
Some king-cup creek;
If Menelaus hung
His head in Egypt
After war was done,
While gnats, then flies, sipped
His blood by night and blistering sun
Until those bony temples held
Ideas that were too brittle, hollow, weak;
As an old parrot tears a rind
From sugary belief —
So, juices of the year
Dry into blacker leaf
And darker fear.

THE FOXY SMELL OF FEAR

I

The foxy smell of fear
    Can change, by a sharp catch of liking,
    Into prim, clear
    Morning snuff, clean as November's
    Bracken after frost.
    And spice-leaves, bruised by blunderers
    In the warm dark, where tree frogs sing
    Like bells on a lost
    Troika trace,
    Are altered and enhanced. Hymettus,
    No. Its honeycombs,
    Paper-thin, are ghostly homes
    Of men whose buzz was disputatious
    In the market-place.

Up the road, cowled in mist,
St. John the Hunter's Church may stare
Over all Athens; and with Attic flair
For moments like Clean Monday, can insist
You bite the sea
Itself and gulp, cold and quick,
Urchin and octopus from the Saronic
Gulf, in true hyperbole.

2

Fisherboys are stretched asleep
  On the seawall of Alexandria.
  Travel, and move further on. Then keep
  Forever in your skull
  That peppered scent
  Of Africa, from the acacia
  And dried grasses. Back at home,
  Brewers' vats, seething
  Black in their digestion, may annul
  The sour and filthy smell
  Of railway fumes
  Which hang near clinkers of embankment
  Slopes, where desperations of poverty
  Once used to roam
  And bindweed has tried living.
  Better invoke
  The hag at Delphi.
  High Parnassian spell
  Or not, kings taken aback
  (So one assumes)
  Or garlanded : power lay in a floor whose stonecrack
  Let out laurel smoke.

VILLAGE SEASONS

A gauzewing fly lights on my hand;
Birds echo; wildest promises abound
And hawthorn creams the land.

Summer, lazing on her elbow,
Watches unremitting mowers, thirsty,
Dazed, work to and fro.

Gold coins — a fortune — drop from trees
Into ditch-coffers underneath the ash
That dangles rusty keys.

Now pumps wear topknots made of straw
And roads clang underfoot; young cheeks shine red,
Bright as a hedge haw.

But cottage Death, huge fisted, wrings
The sheet out when it pleases her, intent,
Intent on other things.

MINIATURE PAEAN

I

When porpoises played to each creaking
Of a clinkered boat and round
The vine-mast Dionysus found,
Men had lined their cheeks from seeking
What can free, exalt, astound;
More were holding back their bile.
The rest, perhaps, could reconcile
Their gods with the hard, mattocked ground.

But now, to feel as proud or blest
As past kings of Vizapore,
Elect in rubies, rich from bézoar,
We must hear ourselves confessed
Because, regardless, we implore
Some power to force the larks to wake,
To keep seas shimmering, and shake
Our own wits sharply, peel and core.

3

However grey Mycenae looks,
The Argive plain gleams ahead,
Golden as Aegisthus' tread;
While, sleepless, travelling in books,
I follow where great names have spread.
A goods train grumbles through the dark;
Soon, quite near, a fox will bark.
Vixen warmth makes a fine bed.

4

Dusty nettles by a farm
Smell good to those who step ashore,
Tired out by sea's hurt and uproar.
With the last grain-sack safe from harm,
Hauled up to lofts, how fine to pour
One's body into freshly tucked
And laundered peace. I've found and sucked
What nourishes, what can restore;

5

Though my stupidity's been grief
Since I have grown from chin to toe.
And yet the cornucopias flow
With music, sea-wrack, insect, leaf,
Well-set page of folio,
Banded snail-shell — for delight,
Awe, pain, ease and fright —
To the mind's high vertigo.

ADAM

Poor Adam ! Marrying
A screech-owl before Eve was made
And liable to meet God walking
Slowly, in the humid, dusky glade.

AN ANSWER FROM DELPHI

I

To keep a balance and to bear
The world; its disarray;
Its wounds; its many failures
Of attempts to supplicate untold
Divergencies of gods angry or gay,
Innocent or shrewd,
By souls a hotch-potch of what is bold,
Eager, alarmed, submissive, wily, crude —
We know such warring humours
Have to be resolved. But where?

2

Beneath a gold mosaic, spanned
By plainchant, resonant with praise
And punishment? Or in
Aeolian islands, ridden by winds, by brightness,
The Bermudas, when a conch shell brays?
Where sages struck a chill
In Ireland's side, through hound, princess
And cattle-thieves, with a strong, holy quill?
Under the salt and skin
Of Jutish estuary land?

3

Parnassos and its rocks resound
With cries of little birds,
Diminished priests of Apollo.
Poverty must work to mule-bells and the clear
Water's tumble. No Castalian words
Are needed to contain
One riddle by another : here,
Sacred and common are conjoined and plain,
While feathery tremors grow
From olive trees clenched in the ground.

COMMON WISH

Love plays in the sun,
Sickens, droops and is done.
A spider's thread
Rolls up, binds up her dead.
There is too much
For us between a dockleaf's touch
And Saturn, which with frosty rings
In utter darkness whirls and stings.

Gleam candour, friend,
Blush to the very end,
Alert and quick
And warm as a hind's lick
Over her calf
To comfort it. Keep near. Then half,
A third, the whole of us could choose
To sop, not crack, our mortal bruise.

WARNING

To be content, you furrow-faced ones,
Your temper
Stinging as radishes,
Hot as boiled onion,
Rough as brown bread;
Relishing the first Isaiah naked,
Preacher of the jostled street —
Keep out of boyhood lanes
Your legs once dawdled in
Or skipped along.

Admissions

1977

ADMISSIONS

Let us then freely admit
That any windfall fruit
May have a wasp in it;

That to hear the word 'fox'
Or see one, prevents an Aran
Fisher putting out;

That Seville's bearers of Passion
Figures, drunk, can shout :
'Your Virgin's a whore !'

That Jachin and Boaz, bronze
Pillars of endurance and might,
Fell with the Temple.

NOT FORGETTING AENEAS SYLVIUS

Not forgetting Aeneas Sylvius —
Novella writer and then Pius the Second —
Gloriously borne aloft
Into the Lateran's basilica
To face a sacristan who knelt
Holding a wisp of burning cotton on a pea-stick :
Totter-man, or throne, needs a reminder
Of how short is triumph,
How it never condescends.

CARPACCIO

St. Ursula dreaming
And the little dog guarding her
Neither are disturbed
By that gentle
Angel of death who opens the door
Quietly

Then on a day
That has each pennant flapping
She embarks on the green sea of Venice
To be martyred in Cologne
Her host of companions
Killed with her

Eleven thousand virgins
Or so it goes
Totally absurd you think
But what a pinprick beside
Each deluded fatuous intake
Of common breath

MUREX

I

Cleopatra the Greek-lipped . . .
Great Alexander gave our country
 To his general.
Pure Macedonian-bred, these Ptolemies
Who've held this Egypt for three hundred years
Or, if you'd sooner, twelve generations
 Of a ruling sister
Married to a brother, as compelled
By Pharaonic, strong official habit.

2

Brilliant and at ease, sure,
 Shrewd in governing
The upper and the lower land whose tongue
She's first of her long line to speak —

Her might, even her magic,
Streams from innate good heart and head.
   Carried among us
She can understand, she hears : brave queen.
   Fit daughter of the sun-god Rê.

3

   She has commanded a shore mollusc
   (From a grey sea-shell)
Crushed by the ton, to give a juice
   So pale, so clear, it shows no colour.
In dim work-lofts, men who steep a stiff,
   Fine-woven cotton in deep troughs
Of it and know the art have found the stuff,
   Nursed away from light,
Seems as if soaked in water, nothing else.

4

Daybreak, and I pressed near when a huge sail
   Was dragged on to open ground.
   The sun glanced,
   Then like a young lover
   Gazed on it till it blushed
   Into astounded purple.
This was to live — to grow as at a trumpet-yell
   Of valour. Then a hymn
Was sung. My chest still feels the ache.

RAPUNZEL

   May I be
   Reminded of Rapunzel;
   Her blue rampion;
   Her prince blinded by thorns
   And how her tears
   Made him fair and whole —
   Each time I meander,
   Stupid with fears,
   Over night's
   Desert of despair.

[117]

CLONMACNOIS

A monastic university founded in the sixth century by St. Ciaran. This centre of scholarship and manuscript-making was repeatedly raided by Danes, then Irishmen, and was finally sacked by the English.

Along the gently
Sloping riverbanks
Of Shannon with its placid flow
And all its wildfowl,
Why should the ruins
Of Clonmacnois,
Pillaged by savages
When most renowned and holy —
Why do its ravages,
In fact,
Make the heart easy
With high calm, tact
And harmony?

MYCENAE

You double lioness of Mycenae
Rearing up each side
Of the male pillar :
Must you guard this gate
To keep alive
The high citadel and the whole story?

Taking fallen rocks
Then adding blood, muscle and flesh
To bones, putting in stomach and heart —
An old man wintering alone
Or the usual peasant nurse
Willing to spin tales
Could do it.

Perhaps a criminal record
Neatly typed
In a police file somewhere
Holds a comparable event.

[118]

But goat-bells on the very spot
Clink out :
This is not so.
Clouds leaning darkly on these mountains,
And the Argive plain, always sunlit,
Equally affirm
That ancestors of Agamemnon
Breathed this air. His family,
Cursed by Pelops,
Made its love and murders
Occupy us now
So that our napes bristle.

REMOTE MATTERS

As long as I can kneel to tell
Pin-eyed from thrum-eyed primroses
Or find a small cranesbill
In rough grass,
Why should I mind
If Dunwich is under the sea
With nine churches drowned?

THE ITALIAN VILLA

All flourished round Tamagno's villa.
'Era più bravo che Caruso, sì,
Perche cantò più forte,'
So a gardener explained.

One day I stood, at noon,
Where shade was blackest under orange-trees
That fruited while they bloomed,
And heard a nightingale.

In full mimosa sun,
This little bird ravished
The ear with a sustained
Precision, finish, delicacy,
And acute surprise.

[119]

VANESSA CARDUI

What human beauties
Pocket Venuses
Can match *Vanessa*

Painted Lady
Fragile
Exquisitely veined

Leaving North
Africa to reach
Ireland

With flirting
Delicate flutter
Of iron obstinacy

WERE THERE A CHOICE

Were there a choice :
The smoothest painted Claude or say
Guercino glade and forest, quiet
As glass, with no twig stirring, not a pulse
Of air, as in a coma
When one scarcely breathes
But feels a calm beyond all telling;
Creatures without help and hounded
As we are, I know — having all but made
That journey to its end —
Such is by far the easiest way to go.

And yet you might prefer
A small, bitter flurry of wind
Battling the tide, its touch pocking
Harbour water into cross-currents and then
Slapping the sea-wall

As you set out, with a stubbed
Dip of dinghy oars — excited
By a smell of kelp, tar,
Wet ropes, half-rusted iron — to the moored
Sailboat waiting for you
With irrevocable, solid planking.

BABY SONG

O cradled daughter :
No Dancing-water
Will make you young
When your dimpled arm
And rounded neck
Look scrawny and wrung.

Provided no harm,
My darling queen,
Should come in between;
No hint of such wreck
As I've suffered and seen.
Now I'll hush my tongue.

Note : *Dancing-water : a fairy elixir to give back lost youth.*

THE OATH

Hand to hand, foot to foot,
Knee to knee, breast to breast
In darkness : a masonic rite.
Would that all lovers
Kept their oath so well.

Notes

page 16   YOUNG ARGONAUTS
The Argonaut legend is probably based on the discovery by
some early Greek expedition which found that the people of
Colchis panned for gold by catching lake water in sheep-
fleeces.

BEAT DRUM, BEAT HEART
   page 26.   'youths To whom a lute, a rose', etc. The sea-
battle of Lepanto in 1571 when the Turks were prevented
from over-running all Europe.

   page 26.   The Chinese Reds' Long March began in October
1934 in Kiangsi (west of Shanghai) with 100,000 men and
ended 368 days later in Shensi (west of Peking) with 50,000
men. They had covered 6,000 miles.

   page 30.   Ronda bridge. An incident in the Spanish civil
war.

   pages 30 *and* 31.   Aldgate and the Minories. A soldier in
Allenby's campaign is speaking.

   page 33.   Brian Boru, King of Munster, was killed in the
eleventh century. It may be remembered that at this time
the Irish were chiefly engaged in fighting the Danes who had
occupied Dublin.

   page 34.   The court cards in some continental packs
represent Rachel, Lancelot, Charles, Judith, Pallas, Lahire,
Hogier, Hector, Alexandre, Caesar, David and Asine.

   page 39.   'But here's a morning walked alone. . .'. This
refers with complete accuracy to the seventh Viscount
Powerscourt and his making of Powerscourt Gardens.

   page 41.   These Pegasi are the heraldic supporters of a
family's coat-of-arms; their bronze models guard this garden's
ornamental lake.

[123]

page 42. The dome of St. Paul's Cathedral houses a library, in a room carved by Grinling Gibbons, where for a few pence one may see one of the finest collections of lay books including this first edition of Chaucer, detailed account-books of the rebuilding of St. Paul's, subscription lists after the Great Fire and many treasures of great interest to biblio-philes. Next door, in the Muniment Room, are the documents and Royal Seals of the early English Kings, many of whom were crowned in old St. Paul's before the Norman Conquest.

The Cathedral used to be the centre of social life for the community and Londoners referred to it as 'our Paul's'. Wren designed the steps leading up to the present building to pre-vent the entry of donkeys loaded with merchandise; but wishing to perpetuate the best of the old tradition he origin-ally planned his Cathedral with small rooms instead of side-chapels, where City Guilds could meet.

page 45. 'By saint', etc. The island of Ensay in the Outer Hebrides is roughly two miles long and half a mile across, but has a very small ruin which is known as St. Columba's Cathedral.

page 45. St. Kevin's hermit cell at Glendalough, a famous tourist sight in Co. Wicklow.

page 46. Fortifications dug up at Megiddo revealed the Biblical 'Armageddon'.

page 53. Erzulie. Voodoo goddess of love in Haitian rites.

page 56. '*Pourrvou*', etc. Favourite remark of Buona-parte's mother when neighbours informed her of her son's victories.

page 56. Excavations at Thermopylae show the truth of Herodotus' statement that the Persian host was so vast that its arrows obscured the sun. The wall of Phocias was found and repairs in it mentioned by Herodotus, also the stone posts of gates from which the name Thermopylae was de-rived. No arrowheads here (from where the Spartans charged the Persians, and Leonidas was killed) but a huge mass of them was found in the hill to which his three hundred withdrew.

page 57. A country legend, in a certain part of France, of Eve and the Garden of Eden.

page 61. Terracotta figures from a tomb in Myrina, of turbaned and dancing winged Erotes, now in the Boston Museum of Fine Arts.

page 78 ARCHITECTURAL TOUR
Clonmacnois. Monastic settlement on the banks of the river Shannon, founded in the sixth century and now a collection of ruins.

page 81 ORIGINS
Trying to discover what ancestors I might have had on both sides of the family who were roughly contemporary in the sixteenth or seventeenth centuries, I came up with the following : (*a*) 'landlord' : a Cornishman, Stephen Braddon of Treworgey St. Gennys, M.P. for Bossiney 1558 to 1565; (*b*) 'peasant' : an Irish cattle-raider successful enough to build himself a small and now demolished castle called Bally Ard in County Offaly in the centre of Ireland; (*c*) 'diplomat' : the Diplomatic Advisor to Ferdinand and Isabella of Spain, some of whose dispatches are still extant; (*d*) 'pedlar' : a Jewish pedlar in the Alsatian town of Colmar.

The following suggestions are taken from Fessenden's *The Deluged Civilization of the Caucasian Isthmus*, whose speculations on the N. Caucasian origin of man as metallurgist have had the support — though for different reasons — of Breasted and Flinders Petrie :

Caspian, Balkasch and Aral Sea are remains, not dried up, of a far larger sea which was once connected with the Arctic Ocean and also, via Manytsch lakes, with Sea of Azov and Black Sea.

When this larger sea was in being, the earliest metal-working civilization was possibly established in N. Caucasus.

Mankind would have had no incentive to leave this locality bounded northward by ice, to the west by a vast morass infested by mosquitoes (Herodotus' 'bees'), to the east by the Everburning Fields (Baku oilfields) and the sea, and to the south by the seemingly impassable range of the Caucasus; also rich in fire (spontaneously ignitable naphtha), metal

[125]

ores, timber, alluvial soil, irrigating streams, useful animals, fruit, grain. Mountain of Iron and Brass nearby (Mt. Thammuzeria or Tamischieria).

With the melting of the ice-cap, the enlarged Caspian (mentioned above) flooded westward and forced discovery of Pass of Dariel (or Erebus) near Mt. Kasbek through the Caucasus and into a region known in Semitic times as Aidon, or more exactly East Aidon.

Erebus, a 500 ft. deep cleft, runs due north and south in lat. 43° so that its forbidding defile is dark even in summer. Its fortified gates (Iron Gates) said to have been placed there by K. Aidoneus (king of Aidon).

Beyond the pass, western and middle portion of valley was called Aidon by Semites, also called Aethiopia by Phoenicians, and later, Colchis by the Greeks. The middle portion, East Aidon — walled in by mountains on all four sides and into which the gate opened — is the *Paradeisos*, or enclosed park, of the Septuagint, and Garden of Eden of Semites. Eastern third of valley, through which R. Alizon flows, called *Elysion* by Greeks.

Vegetation of Garden of Eden luxuriant and dense, with fruit-trees bearing wild fruit, all year round flowers and thick pasturage. Genesis, and Strabo (whose great-uncle was Governor of Colchis) both state very heavy dew watered portion where little rain fell, so never any drought.

Tree of Life; Golden Apples of the Hesperides. Greek tradition says fruit coloured gold and like an apple, prolonging life but guarded by a dragon. Ezekiel says tree guarded by cherubim (Kirubi) with four feet and four wings, like dragons. Creatures which would answer this description are now found in Malaya, in the form of flying lizards : Amagidae, or *draco volans*. They are brightly coloured, look like a snake when their wings are folded, and are partial to *Citrus medica*. 'Upon thy belly thou shalt go' has meaning when applied to these beautiful flying reptiles. *Citrus medica* has remarkable healing properties for wounds; helps the intestinal tract; has a high vitamin content.

Tree of Knowledge of Good and Evil : the thorn-apple (*Daturamatel*) acts like a drug to induce great mental acuity, followed by depression; highly appetizing; an aphrodisiac; can also give violent delirium. Fumes of it when burnt have same effect.

'He placed at the east of the Garden of Eden the Kirubi, and the flame of a sword which turneth every way.' Sword probably a fired oilwell in what is now the Baku district, visible for great distances as it wavered from side to side.

page 87. 'The heart is a small thing, but desireth great matters. It is not sufficient for a kite's dinner, yet the whole world is not sufficient for it.' Anon., twelfth century.

This title quotation is from Quarles' *Emblems,* where it is attributed to Hugo, *Liber de Anima.* The following is an extract from a letter from Fr. A. Gwynn, s.j., of Dublin :

'. . . I have found the very words which Quarles quotes in a treatise *De Interiori Domo,* printed in Migne as a work wrongly attributed to St. Bernard (P.L. 184, col. 543). This treatise is sometimes given as part of *Liber de Anima,* attributed to Hugh of St. Victor. It was probably written by a Cistercian monk of the early twelfth century.

'Here are the words (*loc. sit.*) :

'*De Interiori Domo,* cap. 72 : *O custos cordis, quam modicum et cupidum cor habes! Parvum est et magna cupit. Vix ad unius milvi refectionem sufficere posset, et totus mundus ei non sufficit.*'

page 93 DARKNESS
The family burial-ground is in Powerscourt gardens, a short way from the house. Unkempt, romantic, and beside a ruined church, it is still used by the Wingfield family and their dependents.

page 99 FOR MY DEAD FRIENDS
Asphodel. Most travellers seem disappointed by this plant. They appear not to expect a subdued, rather ghostly, greyish-pink flower.

page 101 REVELATION
'Tinker'. The present dwindling bands of true tinkers are believed to be descendants of people from the Indus Valley

who stayed in the Byzantine Empire, as metal workers, during their slow westward migration.

'Tailor'. Quotations are fragments from Rabbi Hillel, c. 75 BC - 10 AD.

page 109   MINIATURE PAEAN
Stanza 2. *Tavernier's Journals*, ed. of 1678, Bk. II, Chap. 2, says bézoar was a gum secreted by a special breed of Indian she-goat. This substance was thought excessively valuable.